Mid-Life Career Change:
Desire or Necessity?

Mid-Life Career Change: Desire or Necessity?

Teresa Holmes

and

Susan Cartwright

TUDOR

© T. Holmes and S. Cartwright 1996

This version first published in Great Britain by Tudor Business Publishing Limited.

A CIP catalogue record for this book is available from the British Library

ISBN 1 872807 76 3

The right of the authors of this work has been asserted by them in accordance with the Copyright, Designs and Patents Act 1988.

Typeset by Deltatype Ltd, Birkenhead
Printed and bound by Biddles Limited, Guildford, Surrey.

AUTHOR COVERNOTES

Teresa Holmes is a Lecturer in Education and Organizational Psychology at the City of Liverpool Community College. She has had personal experience of radical career change having begun her working life as a secretary.

Dr Susan Cartwright is a Senior Research Fellow and Lecturer in Organizational Psychology at the Manchester School of Management, University of Manchester Institute of Science and Technology. Her early career was spent as a manager in the insurance industry. She is the author of a number of books including most recently Effective Teamworking in the Project Managenent Environment (1995) with Dr Andrew Gale.

ACKNOWLEDGEMENTS

Our thanks to all the individuals who participated in the research and volunteered their experiences. Thanks also to Paula Farr for her patience in producing the manuscript.

CONTENTS

FOREWORD

The nature of work is changing dramatically. More and more organisations are using the dreaded words "outsourcing", "market-testing", "interim management" and the like, which effectively means that many of us will be selling our services to public and private sector organisations on a freelance or short-term contract basis. If this current trend of "privitizing our private sector" continues in the UK, we will increasingly become a nation of blue-collar, white collar, managerial and professional temps. And this trend is extending to Europe, as the need to move toward the convergence of fiscal and monetary policies, and the single currency, drive European companies over the next decade in the direction of part-time working, short-term contracts and less secure organisational careers.

Those who are likely to survive the "virtual" organisation of the future will need to be able to diagnose their abilities and skills to know where to get appropriate training in deficient skills to be able to market themselves to prospective employers and clients; to know how to network; to be able to research the market; to set realistic goals and to create personal marketing plans. The world of business in the future will increasingly move toward individualism in the workplace with employees at all levels taking over the reins of their own careers, as their organisations give them up. Maybe this was always inevitable. Indeed, Walt Whitman once suggested "the whole theory of the universe is directed unerringly to one single individual – namely to you".

This useful book picks up the essence of these trends by attempting to help the individual cope with the ever changing career market and its vagaries. It explores what individuals will need to know about themselves, about the markets, about others and how they will have to plan their career paths for future success. This book is a product of its time and a very useful one at that.

Professor Cary L. Cooper
University of Manchester Institute of Science & Technology (UMIST)
July 1996

INTRODUCTION

"Increasingly people are taking on several unrelated careers per lifetime. Some have been 'restructured' out of companies, but others are motivated by increased life expectancy or a feeling that mid-life achievements have fallen below their aspirations" (Gooding, 1988).

Until relatively recently, a "career for life" was the norm and the principle of "occupational mobility" referred to movement between employers in the pursuit of a higher place on the career ladder. In the 1990s, the position has changed dramatically and there are now many compelling social and economic reasons why individuals may decide or be obliged to consider changing careers at mid-life.

Rapid technological advances combined with organizational changes such as rationalization and delayering have greatly reduced the opportunities for promotion. The "career ladder" now has far fewer rungs, which are harder to climb. These organizational changes often result in more stressful and less fulfilling jobs at a time when people increasingly recognize the importance and value of job satisfaction. Taken together, the uncertainty, pressure and dissatisfying nature of many contemporary jobs has led increasing numbers of people to seek alternative careers. In addition to these voluntary career changes, many individuals are forced to seek alternative occupations because of job losses and a lack of employment opportunities within their current field.

While thirty years ago, only two out of every 100 executives were likely to make a radical career change, during the last decade this figure has risen to 35 per cent (Holmes and Cartwright, 1993). Particularly for those over 35, the most popular career change is towards the autonomy of careers and jobs such as self-employment, lecturing, teaching or consultancy. Between 1979 and 1989, the number of self-employed people in the UK rose by over 70 per cent, from just under 2 million to around 3.25 million. Many individuals who move to self-employment report substantially increased job satisfaction – especially if they are able to turn a hobby into a job.

Unfortunately, this increased desire and need to change career is occurring at a time when many occupations are themselves undergoing radical change. This should not deter prospective career changers; but they do need to adopt a systematic and professional approach to any change they decide to make. Changing career may seem like an interesting but daunting prospect, yet tens of thousands of those who leave Her Majesty's forces each year have been successfully making that transition for years.

Choosing a suitable occupation is always difficult, but especially so for mature adults who feel they cannot afford to make a mistake. Ideally, potential new entrants to an occupation would have the opportunity to gain firsthand experience before making a decision. The mechanisms for doing this do exist (for example job shadowing, temporary appointments, work placements) but are grossly underutilized. In the absence of firsthand experience, it is important to conduct a thorough investigation to see if identified alternative careers are suitable, desirable and available.

Career change may be likened to a maze or a jigsaw: most of the time only a fragmented perspective is possible and the "whole" is hidden from view. The main aim of this book is to help readers to identify the key components of career change which, in turn, should help them to achieve success in their search for a well-matched alternative occupation.

The book is not prescriptive. It does not tell readers what to do but rather advises them on how to do it. This emphasis on self-help is the most effective way to achieve success. To guide readers through the career-change maze the book is divided into four main parts or chapters, each focusing on a particular aspect.

Chapter one identifies self-knowledge as an essential starting point in the desire to set and attain a particular objective. A series of short exercises are provided to help readers to gradually build up a useful profile of: their physical and personality characteristics; their current level of ability, skills and qualifications; and their motivations and expectations. The outcome of these exercises should enable them to identify suitable and desirable alternative occupations.

Chapter two explores ways of investigating the potential market for the characteristics, abilities, qualifications and skills identified in chapter one. This includes a consideration of executing an internal career change (without changing employer) or an external change (by changing employer). Methods of researching markets for alternative occupations are outlined and discussed along with appropriate ways of approaching employers and engaging in effective networking. The intention of this chapter is not to replace the professional advice and guidance available from private and public sector organizations, but to help readers use these facilities more economically and effectively.

Chapter three encourages readers to learn from the experiences of others: to help them identify the key characteristics, processes and circumstances that distinguish a successful career changer from those who have been less successful in their attempts to change career. Case studies of successful and less successful career changers are presented and discussed.

Chapter four emphasizes the role played by planning and preparation in successful career change. Advice is provided on setting realistic goals and systematically working towards these. The importance of regular monitoring, feedback and modification of career-change plans is emphasized and readers are encouraged to find appropriate ways to do this.

Throughout the book the themes of self-knowledge, knowledge of appropriate career markets, and planning and preparation are continually emphasised and reinforced. These are considered the key to successful career change. The principles and practices outlined in the book should provide a solid foundation for identifying appropriate alternative careers and for successfully changing career if this is the intention. Alternatively, the book may make some readers realize that their present state of dissatisfaction is not with their current career but with some aspect of their current employment.

To gain the maximum benefit from the book it is important to read it with an open mind and to continually pose and answer questions with regard to yourself – your current employment, your current career, your current personal circumstances – and to seek solutions to any sources of dissatisfaction that are revealed. One of these solutions may be a change of career: if so you should find the contents of this book both informative and useful.

CHAPTER ONE

KNOW YOURSELF

"Find a job that you like and you'll never work another day in your life"
(Anon).

Knowing yourself is a crucial first step to making an informed decision about career change. Unfortunately, many people find it difficult to conduct an objective self-analysis and rely too much on the opinions of others. These, although important, are no substitute for self-knowledge.

The exercises presented in this chapter provide a simple, speedy and successful route to self-analysis. Each exercise relates specifically to an aspect of self, considered important for self-knowledge, and together they provide a useful starting point for decisions relating to career change or development.

For our purposes, five aspects of self-knowledge have been identified. These are:

Your physical/psychological characteristics

Your working life

Your family commitments/support

Your financial circumstances

Your career-change proposals

For maximum benefit the exercises presented should be tackled quickly and honestly. Where appropriate, check your answers against the scoring systems contained in the appendices. When doing this, it is important to remember that there are no right or wrong answers. The sole aim of the exercises is to help you gain a better understanding of yourself in relation to your career.

YOUR PHYSICAL/PSYCHOLOGICAL CHARACTERISTICS

A candid evaluation of your physical and psychological characteristics is an important step towards self-knowledge. A precise appraisal is neither possible nor necessary. The main aim of this exercise is to provide a general profile against which to match the requirements of selected careers.

Some occupations may have stringent requirements with regard to height, weight, health and fitness. These include jobs with strong physical elements such as the armed forces, police or fire services. If any of your career choices are likely to specify physical requirements it is important to check on these at an early stage to avoid wasting time and risking disappointment at a later stage. If you have any specific health problems it is important to seek medical advice before embarking on a change of job or career that might aggravate these. In addition, it is important to check if a particular medical condition would preclude you from certain careers or make it difficult for you to progress within that career. Physical characteristics are relatively simple to identify and to check against possible new careers. When psychological characteristics are involved the situation is far more complex.

An in-depth personality assessment is not an objective of this book. However, it is useful to identify some of the key factors that determine your behaviour. The psychological characteristics ratings scale has been devised by the authors for this purpose. The scale is built around the five factors thought by many psychologists to explain personality (e.g. McCrae and Costa, 1987).

To avoid the danger of narrow classifications, you are asked to rate yourself against the relevant characteristics on a five point scale ranging

PHYSICAL CHARACTERISTICS			
	Below Average	Average	Above Average
HEIGHT			✔
WEIGHT		✔	
HEALTH		✔	
FITNESS		✔	

from strongly agree to strongly disagree. Once again, there are no right or wrong answers. The responses given are intended to highlight those personality factors most likely to affect your views on particular careers and your suitability for a given career.

Your response to each of the 20 items contained in the psychological characteristics scale should provide a useful insight into your personality (appendix 1). To obtain the maximum benefit from the scale you should analyse your responses in two stages.

Stage One should note responses to individual scale items to provide detailed information on specific aspects of your personality (e.g. whether you are prone to stress, like working independently, or dislike teamwork).

Stage Two should group the responses to associated clusters of items together to provide a more factorized profile of your personality (e.g. if you have low scores for Section A you would be classified as an introvert; if you have high scores for Section C you are open to new experiences).

Taken together, these two stages should serve as useful indicators of your dominant personality characteristics.

In addition, it is also possible to build up a crude personality profile by comparing responses to different sections. For example, a tendency towards introversion may be attributable to a strong desire for independence, a lack of assertiveness, or lack of self-confidence. A tendency towards conformity (a low score on Section D) may be due to timidity and fear of reprisals or to a belief in the necessity of following rules and regulations wherever possible. Once you have discovered your key personality characteristics the information can be used to identify careers that most closely match these. The following examples illustrate how such matching could occur.

Someone who enjoys working as part of a team and feels they have a duty to help others, would appear well suited to one of the caring professions such as nursing, teaching or social work.

A strong preference for independence may indicate a suitability for self-employment.

A preference for "facts" and working alone may suggest a career in computers.

PSYCHOLOGICAL CHARACTERISTICS RATINGS SCALE

INSTRUCTIONS: Below are 20 items organized under five sections. On a scale of 1 to 5: 1 = strongly agree; 2 = agree; 3 = uncertain; 4 = disagree; 5 = strongly disagree. Circle the number that most closely expresses your response to each item (e.g. if you AGREE with Item 1 put a circle around the response choice 2).

Section A	Response		Choice		
1. I do not like working in a team	1	2	③	4	5
2. I do not make friends very easily	1	2	3	4	⑤
3. I usually adopt a serious approach to life	1	②	3	4	5
4. I am usually fairly resourceful	①	2	3	4	5
Section B					
5. I tend to get hurt and upset very easily	1	2	③	4	5
6. I often feel tense and find it hard to relax	1	2	3	4	⑤
7. I am usually described as a 'worrier'	1	②	3	④	5
8. I have a very low stress threshold	1	2	3	4	⑤
Section C					
9. I do not like too much change in my life	1	2	3	4	⑤
10. I usually obey rules and regulations	①	2	3	4	5
11. I prefer routine, predictable work	1	2	③	4	5
12. I usually accept the decisions of others	1	2	③	4	5
Section D					
13. I dislike arguing with people	1	2	③	4	5
14. I always try to be pleasant and courteous	①	2	3	4	5
15. I do not like to criticise or discipline people	1	2	③	4	5
16. I like to help others whenever possible	①	2	3	4	5
Section E					
17. I always try to be reliable and trustworthy	①	2	3	4	5
18. I am always a careful, methodical worker	1	2	③	4	5
19. I work hard at all my tasks	1	2	③	4	5
20. I am very persistent	1	2	③	4	5

A desire to conform may suit occupations where obeying rules and regulations is important, such as the police, armed forces or the legal profession.

A tendency towards creativity, non-conformity, and a dislike of routine may indicate the attraction of a career in the arts or media.

An extrovert personality may be well suited to a career as a salesperson.

Increased awareness of your physical and psychological characteristics is only the first step towards knowing yourself. The exercises you have completed as part of the first section of this chapter are useful in relation to all aspects of your life although the main aim of the book is to help you to identify a suitable career. The next section narrows the focus by concentrating specifically on self-awareness in relation to your working life.

YOUR WORKING LIFE

The importance of continually updating a curriculum vitae is widely acknowledged, if not so widely practised. However, less attention is given to the need for a periodic audit or personal stocktake of abilities, experiences, qualifications and personal preferences in the work environment. Initial career decisions are typically based on incomplete information and little real knowledge of what the day to day work involves (Cartwright and Cooper, 1994). Early career choices are often influenced by factors such as parental or peer pressure, images portrayed by the media, high starting salaries and attractive perks or glossy recruitment literature, rather than aptitude and personality. Career satisfaction is therefore often a matter of chance rather than choice. However, even if a good choice is made initially, a career can often become inappropriate or dissatisfying as different stages in the life cycle are reached and attitudes and values change. Redundancy can therefore present an opportunity for re-appraisal, and a chance to make a fresh and invigorating new start.

As part of the personal audit process, it is useful to consider the following:

ability – levels of competence, proficiency, expertise or skill in the performance of mental or physical acts that may be useful in your working life;

qualifications – any awards, credit, certificates etc., that may be useful in your working life;

experience – a wide range of events and occurrences from different aspects of your life that may be useful in the workplace. These would include experiences relating to the home, voluntary work or hobbies.

When carrying out such an audit, it is advisable to include your entire repertoire of abilities, experiences and qualifications rather than focus only on those considered relevant to your present job and career. The completed audit will enable you to identify those items which are currently not utilized or under-utilized but which may be important assets in other occupations.

Look back over your audit and tick off the abilities, experiences and qualifications most frequently used in your current job. If most or all of these are fully utilized perhaps it is another aspect of your present job or career that is causing dissatisfaction. However, if you find that many of your capabilities are under-utilized it is likely that your current job and/or career are unsuitable and a better "match" should be sought.

It is also important to consider what you liked or disliked about your current or previous jobs and the type of working environment that you prefer. For example, do you prefer a working environment with a high team spirit; or where there is opportunity to get out and meet people; or is close to home? It can also be useful to consider past opportunities which you regret not taking.

Other factors likely to affect the level of satisfaction with a job or career are the psychological characteristics referred to earlier in this chapter. Look back at these and compare and contrast them with the outcome of the more recent audit. If obvious discrepancies are apparent it might be useful to spend some time considering if these are serious enough to warrant a job or career change. Two aspects of working life which are crucial to satisfaction and fulfilment are motivation and locus of control.

MOTIVATION

Motivation is the term generally employed to explain the phenomena

AUDIT OF QUALIFICATIONS, EXPERIENCES AND SKILLS		
Abilities (e.g. interpersonal, numerical, verbal, listening...)	Experiences (e.g. running a home, supervising a production line, running an amateur football team...)	Qualifications (e.g. RSA typing, A level Maths, GCSE English...)

concerned in the operation of incentives, drives and motives (Driver, 1979). In a similar way, "motivation" refers to the regulation of need satisfaction and goal-striving behaviour (Hilgard, et al., 1973).

If we posed the question "why do people work?" the most common response would be "to ensure economic survival". Recognizing this, a more fruitful line of questioning would be to find out what motivates people in their current occupation. Research indicates that work-related motivation is a complex issue with multiple motives the norm (Holmes and Cartwright, 1995). Given this, the most useful approach to investigating self-motivation is to help people identify the priority they give to work-related motives.

The Motivation Priority Scale is an adapted version of a scale devised to investigate the main motives for mid-career change among managers and professionals (Holmes and Cartwright, 1995). This adapted version focuses on ranked motives to help readers prioritise what they want from a job in relation to their current occupation. In addition, if a career change is imminent or under serious consideration, the scale can also be used to help identify the direction a career change should take.

To guard against excessive influence from temporary, situational factors it is advisable to complete the scale on more than one occasion. A comparison of responses obtained on these different occasions will enable you to identify any inconsistencies among ranked items. Slight variations in priority should be expected but if radical changes are noted then the reasons for these would need to be explored. Scoring details for the Motivation Priority Scale are provided in appendix 2. The scoring key provided in appendix 2 indicates whether your work-related motives generally reflect internal values (from within yourself) or external values (from outside yourself). Examples of internal values would include a desire for job satisfaction or fulfilment, opportunities for greater use of initiative and creativity and a desire for full skill-utilization. Examples of external values would include a desire for job security, financial rewards, status and promotion.

It is unlikely that individuals will be motivated entirely by internal or external values, but usually by a combination of both. However, it should be possible to see if internal or external motives predominate. In addition, the reasons behind the motives need to be explored to discover the role played by situational factors such as job insecurity, unemployment, family pressure or financial difficulties.

MOTIVATION PRIORITY SCALE	
Instructions: Make a list of the things which are important to you in your present occupation. Examples of requirements you might include are making useful contacts, good opportunities for promotion, high financial rewards, and a sense of achievement. When you have completed your list, place them in order of priority. Items should be ranked in descending order from 1 to 12 with 1 representing your highest priority and 12 your lowest.	
Item	Rank

LOCUS OF CONTROL

Locus of control is a generalized expectancy that rewards, reinforcements or outcomes in life are controlled by our own actions (internality) or by other forces (externality) (Spector, 1988).

Faced with major life events, Murgatroyd (1988) argues there are three main coping strategies available to solve problems that arise. These are: (i) to change the situation; (ii) to redefine the meaning of the situation; (iii) to cope with an experience when it happens.

The most effective and least stressful approach is to move between the three strategies as appropriate. However, to be able to do this, an individual would need to feel in control of his or her life.

Individual differences in locus of control are usually measured by scores on a rating scale. Early locus of control scales (Rotter, 1966) measured an individual's generalized expectancies for internal or external locus of control. Later scales (for example Levenson, 1974) split locus of control into a variety of factors (such as personal life, social, political, etc.) measured by separate scales. Most appropriate for present purposes is a work-related locus of control scale devised by Spector (1988).

Locus of control is an important element of both satisfaction with an existing job and career, and the type of new job or career sought by an individual. The Spector Locus Of Control Scale will help you to measure your own locus of control. Once again, your response to scale items may be influenced to some extent by situational factors. To counteract this, it is advisable to complete the scale on more than one occasion and compare your overall scores. If more than a slight difference is noted, it is useful to compare the scores for individual items and seek explanations for any major differences that are found. Scoring details for the Spector Locus of Control Scale are provided in appendix 3. Before you complete and score the scale it might be useful to speculate on the extent to which you feel you are internally or externally controlled. This should prove an interesting exercise in self-analysis.

Locus of control is an important factor in job and career satisfaction. Individuals with a high internal locus of control need to feel in control of their working lives and would be unhappy in a job or career that did not fulfil this need. Alternatively, individuals with a high external locus of control may feel more comfortable in a job or career where others exerted control.

It may be interesting to compare and contrast the result from the Motivation and Spector Locus of Control Scales to see if there is any link between "motivation" and "locus of control", for example, to see if an individual with a high internal locus of control is motivated by

---

SPECTOR LOCUS OF CONTROL SCALE

Below are 16 items. Please mark each item 1-6 according to the extent to which you agree or disagree with the statement made. The choices are: 1 = disagree very much; 2 = disagree moderately; 3 = disagree slightly; 4 = agree slightly; 5 = agree moderately; 6 = agree very much.

1. A job is what you make of it...

2. On most jobs people can pretty much accomplish whatever they set out to accomplish...

3. If you know what you want out of a job, you can find a job that gives it to you..

4. If employees are unhappy with a decision made by their boss, they should do something about it...

5. Getting the job you want is mostly a matter of luck..........

6. Making money is primarily a matter of good fortune........

7. Most people are capable of doing their jobs well if they make the effort..

8. In order to get a really good job you need to have family members or friends in high places...

9. Promotions are usually a matter of good fortune..............

10. When it comes to landing a really good job, who you know is more important that what you know..

11. Promotions are given to employees who perform well on the job...

12. To make a lot of money you have to know the right people...

13. It takes a lot of luck to be an outstanding employee on most jobs...

14. People who perform their jobs well generally get rewarded for it...

15. Most employees have more influence on their supervisors then they think they do..

16. The main difference between people who make a lot of money and people who make a little money is luck...

14

internal values such as job satisfaction and fulfilment, use of initiative and creativity and self-actualization. Alternatively, an individual with a high external locus of control may also be more motivated by external values such as high financial rewards, job perks and status.

An important aspect of any psychological concept is how individuals perceive themselves. If there was a marked discrepancy between your perceived and actual locus of control it is worth investigating further. The work-based nature of the Spector Locus Of Control Scale may mean that scores are heavily influenced by personal experience (Holmes and Cartwright, 1995). For instance, in some organizations promotions are rarely based on merit and this is likely to influence the responses of people who work (or have worked) for this type of employer. If you suspect this to be the case check individual scale items to identify which ones have influenced your overall score in the direction under dispute. However, discrepancies may indicate a lack of self-understanding in this area.

An understanding of motivation and locus of control is an important part of understanding what makes you like or dislike a particular job or career. In addition, it should prove invaluable if a change of direction is required.

However, people can rarely afford the luxury of selecting a job or career purely on the basis of personal preference or suitability. Other factors also have to be taken into consideration. Two such factors are family commitments and support and financial circumstances. These are considered in the following sections.

YOUR FAMILY COMMITMENTS/SUPPORT

Research indicates (Holmes and Cartwright, 1994; Holmes and Cartwright, 1995) that workers are becoming increasingly concerned with their personal lives and are striving to achieve a better balance between their working and personal lives. This change is largely attributable to noticeable increases in pressure at work; stress levels; concern with health and fitness; opportunities for leisure pursuits and average life span.

This change in value towards personal development has occurred at a time when job security and opportunities for advancement have decreased. Rationalization within organizations has meant greatly increased pressure for staff who remain. An increased workload and longer working week make it difficult for workers to enjoy their leisure time. At the same time, job insecurity deters complaints and the pursuit of "career development" is often replaced by the fight for "job survival".

Against this background an increasing number of workers contemplate a change of occupation. In many instances they are forced to consider a career change because of limited job opportunities within their existing occupation; in others a change is voluntarily sought. If a change in direction is contemplated, family circumstances should be considered before any firm decisions are made. Family circumstances need to be considered from two viewpoints: commitments and support.

FAMILY COMMITMENTS

Family commitments comprise responsibilities to family members such as spouse, children, parents and siblings. This would include typical commitments such as the provision of financial security, companionship, moral obligations and support. In addition, in some instances the commitment may be greater, such as the need to provide care for a family member with a serious medical condition or emotional problem.

It is very difficult to quantify family commitments in terms of time and money. However, some estimation may be required if a contemplated career change is likely to be accompanied by radical changes in the amount of time or money available for your family. There is no easy way to quantify family commitment but suggestions made in this section should prove useful in either their present format or an adapted version of this.

One way to quantify family commitments is to analyse them in terms of their nature and the time devoted to them. The following tables present examples of how this analysis can be carried out. If the suggested headings are inappropriate to your own circumstances then adapt the headings accordingly. Once compiled, the content of the tables should prove a useful way of confronting your present and future family commitments.

By specifying actual family members, the nature of the commitment involved, and how this is likely to change in the short and longer-term,

THE NATURE OF FAMILY COMMITMENTS			
Family Member	Nature of the commitment	Expected short-term changes	Expected longer-term changes
Examples			
Daughter	GCSE exams	Pass	A levels
Mother	Hospital visits	Home support	Recovery

the scale of individual and total commitments become apparent. Although the "changes" specified may be only estimates, they should provide a useful indication of the level of commitment required over specified periods of time. The following examples help to illustrate how the table may be used.

Example One: the nature of the commitment might relate to two children, one aged 10 and the other aged 16. Over at least the next six years the younger child would require schooling but the older child may leave school and achieve financial independence or continue into further and higher education requiring continued financial support. A knowledge of the plans of the older child should be taken into account when planning a career change. In addition, the younger child may need to remain at a particular school thus limiting geographical mobility.

Example Two: the nature of the commitment might relate to an elderly parent who had recently suffered a stroke. Their chance of complete or partial recovery should be considered in the short and longer term if this would affect any career change decisions.

Although the nature of family commitments is important they should not be considered in isolation. Equally important is the time that needs to be devoted to these commitments and the time remaining that could be used for other types of commitment. The table below indicates how existing time commitments can be measured and "free time" identified. The above timetable should only be used as a rough guide to when and

TIME CURRENTLY DEVOTED TO FAMILY COMMITMENTS			
	Morning	Afternoon	Evening
Monday			
Tuesday			
Wednesday			
Thursday			
Friday			
Saturday			
Sunday			

how long you devote to particular family commitments in a "typical" week. Some of these fixtures will be fairly rigid, others more flexible. It is important to identify these and to use this information to estimate how much "free time" is available if this is needed for working towards or in a new career. The most likely time commitments when working towards a new career include information gathering, training or studying, job search and preparation. The most likely time commitments when starting a new career include preparation for work, additional work commitments, additional travel time and time spent away from home.

FAMILY SUPPORT

Family support is usually needed if radical changes in family life are involved. This is even more difficult to quantify than family commitments, but it is useful to consider the type of changes likely to result from any change of occupation, how long these are likely to last and how they would affect the different members of your family. The nature and extent of support needed will depend largely on the nature and extent of the changes taking place. Examples of possible changes and required support should help to illustrate these points.

Example One: a new career would involve longer commuting distances. Public transport is not a viable proposition and your spouse normally uses the car. You calculate that you either need the car every day or you need to be driven to a railway station every day. The support of your spouse is obviously vital if your transport problems are to be resolved.

Example Two: a new career would involve regular trips abroad. This would cause serious disruptions to family life. The support of the whole family would be needed to avoid discord.

Example Three: a new career would involve entertaining clients at home without disruptions. Support from your immediate family together with parents and in-laws might be needed to ensure children are cared for and do not disrupt your dinner parties.

Once you have identified the nature and extent of family support needed to successfully change occupation, this should be discussed with the appropriate family member(s) at an early stage in your career-change plans. If the required support is unlikely to be forthcoming then perhaps the proposed change needs to be reconsidered. It is important not to underestimate the role played by the various family members in your working life and the need for their support in any new venture under consideration.

You may have noticed that one crucial aspect of family commitment and support has been largely neglected so far, namely financial. This is not an oversight. The importance and complexity of financial circumstances warrant a separate section.

YOUR FINANCIAL CIRCUMSTANCES

Before embarking on a job or career change it is crucial to carefully consider your financial circumstances. This would include not only your present circumstances but any changes that are likely to occur within the short and longer term. The following categories provide a useful framework within which to analyse the financial aspects of a job or career change. The implications of any proposed changes can then be considered.

INCOME AND EXPENDITURE

All current regular income should be recorded based on weekly, monthly or annual earnings (whichever is most appropriate or convenient). This should include contributions from all relevant members of the household. Other, more periodic forms of income should then be estimated. A similar exercise should be carried out in relation to current expenditure, separating essential and non-essential spending.

Regular or periodic savings should also be taken into account together with any interest earned through savings. Examples of savings should include money deposited in banks, building societies or post offices, government bonds or savings certificates, share ownership, unit trusts, and income-bearing insurance policies.

Likely changes in income and expenditure should be projected over a one, three and five year period taking into account expected changes in family circumstances. These may include children attaining financial independence, the need to support children at college or university, a partner returning to paid employment, or the completion of repayments on a mortgage or loan.

OTHER FINANCIAL ASPECTS OF CURRENT EMPLOYMENT

In some jobs, non-salary financial aspects may have a crucial bearing on whether or not an alternative job or career is viable. These would include the various "perks" offered by employers such as bonuses, commission, cheap or free health cover, travel allowance, company car and company pension scheme. In addition, employees may receive discounts on the products or services produced by their company.

When considering your current financial circumstances it is crucial to take account of job perks. Without these, it is likely your expenditure would greatly increase adversely affecting the balance between the income and expenditure worked out in the previous section of this chapter. It may be necessary for a new job or career to provide similar types of perks to make it worthwhile changing to them. Even if this is not the case, a full picture of current income and expenditure is necessary to enable you to make informed decisions.

TRAINING COSTS

If a career change is proposed it is possible that some form of training or retraining programme will be needed to meet the requirements of the new occupation. It may be possible to make use of training facilities and opportunities provided by an existing employer prior to the change. This is particularly relevant if a career change is planned well in advance. Alternatively, free courses sponsored by various government agencies might be available or the local authority might be prepared to fund your studies. It is also worth checking with local banks regarding the availability and terms of Career Development Loans.

However, depending on the type of training programme required it may be necessary to fund this yourself. If so, would fees need to be paid in full initially or could they be paid in instalments? Enquiries concerning costs and financial assistance should be made prior to committing yourself to a course or programme. This is particularly important if a full-time course is involved.

Even if funding is available you need to consider the time required to complete the course. This would include study time as well as organized attendance. The time devoted to a course or programme of study should be offset against alternative uses of that time, such as earning additional income or home commitments.

TRAVEL COSTS

Travel costs are a major factor in job or career change decisions if the proposed change involves a major geographical upheaval. If a new employer is located within travelling distance of the existing family home then it is necessary to calculate any increase in travel time and costs that might be incurred. This needs to be considered before accepting a new position. The difficulties involved in making the journey should also be considered; for example, public transport facilities, wear and tear on a car, petrol costs, winter weather. All these factors could add to the pressure of a new job.

In some instances, the geographical distance may to too great to commute to work from the existing family home. In this case you would either have to live away from home during working days returning at weekends and holidays or relocate the family to the new area. Both solutions have attendant problems. Living away from home is expensive (accommodation and travel costs in addition to the upkeep of the family home) and a strain on family relationships. Relocating the family is also expensive (especially if house prices differ considerably between areas) and involves separating family members from relatives and friends. Further relocation problems may arise if children are at a crucial stage of their education or if they or your partner have jobs in the existing area.

COMPENSATING FOR FINANCIAL CHANGES

If financial constraints appear to be a deterrent to a job or career change, ways to compensate for any loss of income need to be considered. The first question to ask is: "how long will a reduced income be necessary?" If the reduction is temporary and the new job or career will eventually be more financially rewarding then the initial sacrifices might be relatively easy to make. However, if the new job or career offers no prospect of a return to existing income levels the decision to change needs more careful consideration. If a change is still necessary or desirable then ways to compensate for long-term income reduction should be sought.

Additional income could be found in a variety of ways. Other members of the family could contribute more of their income (if possible), second jobs could be taken, or the possibility of some form of income support could be investigated.

Alternatively, ways of reducing the family budget could be explored. The importance of splitting expenditure into "essential" and "non-essential" items is now apparent. Another way of reducing expenditure is to look for cheaper versions of essential items and to reduce costs where wastage often occurs (such as gas, electricity and telephone). Car sharing could also be considered with passengers contributing to petrol costs.

A careful and detailed consideration of your financial circumstances – both immediate and in the longer term – is an essential element of any proposal to change job or career. Having considered all the main variables along the lines suggested it is appropriate to ask yourself two important questions before proceeding: "can I afford to change job or career now or in the immediate future?" and "would my family support any job or career change I decided to make?"

The latter question is a reminder that decisions to change job or career cannot be taken in a vacuum. If other people are affected by your decision they need to be considered. The commitment and support of your immediate family (explored in the previous section of this chapter) are crucial if a job or career change is to succeed. This is particularly true if financial resources and security are adversely affected by this change.

The complex nature of a job or career change should now be apparent. This is explored in the final section of this chapter which focuses on decision making and the implications of any decisions you might make.

YOUR CAREER CHANGE PROPOSALS

It is now time to apply the self knowledge gained from working through this chapter. By the end of this section you should be ready to answer two fundamental questions: "should I change career?" and, if so, "what direction should this career change take?"

PRESENT CAREER

Viewing your "career" from an historical perspective is a useful device when considering a change of occupation. Spend a few moments contemplating the progression of your career to date and present this in the form of a flowchart. This should include key "stageposts" such as first job, subsequent jobs, promotions, past career changes, and finish with your current (or last) work position. The exercise should then be repeated to project where you expect to be in three, five and ten years' time.

When you have prepared your "career progression" flowchart, analyse your current career in terms of its most and least attractive characteristics. List these on a chart (see example).
Having identified the most and least attractive characteristics of your current career you should further identify those that relate specifically to your career as a whole and your current (or last) job. This is important since the source of dissatisfaction may lie with a particular job rather than with a career. If this is the case, then it may be possible to

CURRENT CAREER CHARACTERISTICS		
Current Career	**Most Attractive Characteristics**	**Least Attractive Characteristics**
Examples:		
Sales Rep	Flexible hours	Irregular income
Teacher	Long holidays	Bureaucracy

restructure or adapt the job to make it better suited to your needs. If this is not possible then a change of employer or move to self-employment should be considered. If the career itself is the cause of dissatisfaction then a change of occupation may be necessary.

New career

When considering a new career, a good starting point is to draw up a list of all possible job and career alternatives that could be of interest and rank them in terms of the degree of interest, knowledge and experience they represent to you. It is also important to clarify expectations in relation to that career. The Expectations Priority Scale is an adaptation of a scale used to investigate differences in expectations between successful and unsuccessful career changers (Holmes and Cartwright, 1995). Twelve popular "expectations" have been listed. However, if there are other, more appropriate expectations you wish to add in relation to your own career plans, please do so in the spaces provided. Once again, it is advisable to complete this scale on more than one occasion to guard against temporary, situational factors. Scoring details for this scale are provided in appendix 4.

Your response to the items presented in the Expectations Priority Scale are indicators of what you would require from any new career on which you embarked. In addition, the scoring key provided in Appendix 4

EXPECTATIONS PRIORITY SCALE		
Instructions: Below are twelve items. Please rank these in order of priority in relation to your expectations of a new career. Items should be ranked in descending order from 1 to 12 with '1' representing your highest priority and '12' your lowest.		
Item		**Rank**
1.	A wider variety of work tasks to perform	
2.	A higher level of occupational status	
3.	Increased prospects for promotion	
4.	Improved opportunities for continued training	
5.	More autonomy/opportunity to use initiative	
6.	A higher level of job fulfilment/satisfaction	
7.	Increased financial rewards	
8.	An increase in job-related perks and general conditions of service	
9.	A greater sense of identity with the new role(s)/tasks	
10.	An improved personal life	
11.	A higher level of participation in decision-making	
12.	More meaningful/worthwhile tasks to perform	
13.	....	
14.	....	

identifies the internal or external nature of your career change expectations. Examples of internal expectations would include the desire for increased job fulfilment/satisfaction, greater autonomy/opportunity to use initiative and to have more meaningful/worthwhile tasks to perform. Examples of external expectations would include a desire for increased financial rewards, promotion prospects and a higher level of occupational status. Most people will have a combination of internal and external expectations but the emphasis they place on these will differ as indicated by the priority allocated to particular scale items.

PURSUING OBJECTIVES

When pursuing a new career it is usual to encounter a number of factors

	THE FACILITORY/INHIBITORY RATINGS SCALE
	Instructions: the following twelve items describe factors that may facilitate or inhibit career change. Read each item carefully and respond to it according to your own career change experiences and expectations. Only ONE response may be made for each item. The response categories are: 1 - strongly agree; 2 = agree; 3 = uncertain; 4 = disagree; 5 = strongly disagree
1.	Education and training provision will assist career change..........
2.	Employers generally have a positive attitude towards career change............
3.	Past failures are likely to act as a deterrent to subsequent career change attempts.........
4.	Ample opportunities exist for those wanting to change career........
5.	Family and close relatives will generally be supportive of attempts to change career.......
6.	The rigid nature of most pension schemes is likely to act as a deterrent to voluntary career change.......
7.	Financial restrictions are a serious deterrent to career change.......
8.	The degree of family responsibility decreases with age thus making it easier to change career as we get older........
9.	The lack of relevant qualifications and/or work experience is likely to restrict movement between careers........
10.	The current facilities for career guidance and counselling are inadequate and restrict opportunities for change....
11.	The possibility of making a successful career change tends to decrease with age.....
12.	The encouragement and support of family, friends and colleagues is likely to make career change easier......
13.	....

which will either assist or hinder you in the achievement of your objective. The Facilitatory/Inhibitory Ratings Scale was designed (Holmes and Cartwright, 1995) to help assess attitudes towards such factors. Once again, common "facilitators" and "obstacles" have been listed. However, further more appropriate examples may be added (and scored) if you wish. Scoring details for this scale are provided in Appendix 5. As with the earlier scales, it is advisable to complete the scale on more than one occasion to guard against situational factors.

The scoring key outlined in appendix 5 should provide insight into the positive or negative way you approach a change of occupation. Given the difficulties associated with a career change it is usual to recognize factors likely to hinder progress. However, some people will be more pessimistic about these difficulties than others and emphasize them more strongly than factors likely to assist career change.

Individuals with a mainly positive approach to career change will emphasize factors such as the education and training facilities available, the positive attitude of employers and the support available to help them change career. Those with a generally negative attitude towards career change will emphasize factors such as inadequate advice and guidance, financial restrictions and rigid pension schemes acting as deterrents to career change.

MATCHING PSYCHOLOGICAL CHARACTERISTICS TO A NEW CAREER

The more self-knowledge you have, particularly in relation to your work-based motives and expectations, the easier it will be to choose an appropriate alternative career. This important issue will be returned to in later chapters, but a provisional mention is relevant here.

Most people have complex needs which cannot be satisfied entirely through their occupation. However, since we spend so much of our waking lives at work, it is important to seek jobs which can satisfy many or most of our work-related needs.

If responses to the self-assessment exercises have indicated that your career needs relate mainly to external influences (such as financial rewards, job perks, status, promotion prospects, working conditions, etc.) then the work content of an occupation is likely to be of secondary importance. If this is the case, then an alternative career should be selected (primarily) on the basis of how well it satisfies these requirements.

Alternatively, if internal aspects of a career (such as job satisfaction/ fulfilment, greater identity with the job, more provision for autonomy and creativity, etc.) are paramount then the work content of an occupation will assume greater importance. Examples of "career matching" in such instances are provided.

Example One: a desire for greater autonomy/independence at work. Individuals who value autonomy and independence might be suited to self-employment, or jobs which are not closely supervised (such as sales representatives, teachers/lecturers, tradesmen, auditor, etc.).

Example Two: a desire for greater creativity. If flair and creativity are important components of a job then careers which provide scope for self-expression and individualism need to be targeted. These are wide-ranging and include hairdressing, dressmaking, journalism, public relations, advertising, marketing, floristry, window dresser, artist, designer (fashion, graphic, interior, etc.), photographer, performer (actor, musician, dancer, etc.), make-up artist, etc.

Example Three: a desire for a more worthwhile job. Individuals for whom this is important would need to determine exactly what is "worthwhile" to them. As a general rule, some form of "caring" or "helping" occupation may be suitable. These would include nursing, teaching, social work, work for a charitable institution, community worker, careers advisor, religious minister, etc.

Example Four: a desire for greater job identity and involvement. This would apply to many of the occupations already mentioned. For example, it would apply to jobs involving team work (such as nursing, social work, advertising, marketing, market research, town planning, managers, personnel and training, etc.); or jobs with responsibility for people or resources (such as supervisory or managerial).

Example Five: a desire to work alone. Most jobs involve some degree of social interaction. However, there are some occupations where the main emphasis is on the "task" rather than on interacting with people (either other staff, customers or clients). Examples of such jobs would include laboratory technician, scientist, technical writer, computer engineer, computer programmer, systems analyst, archivist, electrician, bricklayer, architect, accountant, etc.

Example Six: a desire for greater job satisfaction/fulfilment. Once again, "satisfaction and fulfilment" will vary with individuals and it is important to discover exactly what type of occupations and tasks would satisfy these requirements. If "creativity" produces these feelings then an occupation which provided opportunities for creativity/innovation should be selected. Alternatively, if "helping others" provides satisfaction/fulfilment one of the "caring or helping" professions should be considered.

As you can see, identifying an "ideal" or "well–matched" occupation is very difficult. The best way to approach this task is to select occupations that appear to meet most or many of your work-related needs and investigate these more closely to see if they would be suitable alternative careers. As mentioned earlier, this complex issue is targeted again in later chapters.

The results of the final self-analysis exercises contained in this section should provide the final piece of the "know yourself" jigsaw. Hopefully, you are now in a position to identify one or more alternative careers. The remainder of this book focuses on how to pursue and achieve the career change you propose.

CHAPTER TWO

KNOW YOUR MARKET

Knowing your market is the next logical step to knowing yourself. The exercises contained in chapter one should have developed your powers of systematic self-analysis and provided a useful indication of the direction a career change might take.

Chapter two focuses on how to research the potential markets you have identified to discover the opportunities for new entrants with your qualifications, skills and experience. The chapter is divided into six sections:

Exploring suitable career options

Internal v external career change

Researching the market

Contacting organizations

Effective networking

Sources of career advice and guidance

These sections provide a framework within which to explore the feasibility of specific career options. They are not meant to be restrictive, exhaustive or rigid. The key to any type of change is "flexibility" and this should be borne in mind when working through this chapter.

EXPLORING SUITABLE CAREER OPTIONS

An audit of your qualifications, abilities and work experience together with a knowledge of what you would expect from a new career are useful indicators of the general direction a career change should take. However, they are less useful in guiding you towards a specific new occupation.

Various reference books listing classifications of careers are available for consultation. An early, detailed classification of occupations in terms of their focus of activity and level of function within these is provided by Roe (1956) who emphasizes the importance of career choice to meet the diverse needs of individuals. The major classification groups identified by Roe are: professional and managerial; clerical and sales; service; agricultural, forestry and kindred occupations; skilled; semi-skilled; and unskilled. Each of the major classifications comprises various sub-classifications based on the levels within an occupation group. A similarly detailed classification was compiled by Holland (1973).

Generally accessible careers classifications and job descriptions are included in *Occupations* (an annual directory of 600 jobs with simple job descriptions and training notes); *Working In* (a series of booklets providing insight into the day-to-day activities of various occupations); *Your GCSE Decisions* (which includes a classification of courses); *What Do Graduates Do?* (occupational choices for graduates) and *Second Chances* (information on careers). Further information on these publications is provided in appendix 6.

A general summary of occupations is provided in appendix 7. Before progressing further it would be useful to read through these and provisionally identify those occupations you feel are particularly suitable in the light of your self-analysis from chapter one. It would be unwise to target only one new occupation at this stage. The most sensible approach is to initially identify several desirable occupations and investigate each in terms of its viability. Following such investigations the most feasible option(s) should be targeted for more detailed attention.

A good way to start the elimination process is to carry out a personal SWOT analysis by examining your Strengths, Weaknesses, Opportunities and Threats in relation to each of the possible new occupations. Three sample SWOT analyses are provided to assist you in this task.

Example One: change of occupation from sales manager to accountant

Strengths

1.   an aptitude for figures

2.   a liking for routine tasks

3.   strong family support

Weaknesses

1. age (over 50)

2. limited financial resources

3. restricted geographical mobility

Opportunities

1. large number of vacancies for qualified accountants

2. assistance with fees whilst training

Threats

1. age prejudice by employers

2. most of the vacancies outside your region

3. the long training period favours younger candidates

Example Two: change of occupation from van driver to self-employed chauffeur

Strengths

1. ten years employment experience as a driver

2. good interpersonal skills

Weaknesses

1. recent driving offences mean the absence of a clean driving licence

2. poor time management skills

Opportunities

1. TEC initiatives to encourage self-employment

2. the novelty factor of being a "female" chauffeur

Threats

1. competition from self-employed male chauffeurs

2. a large established car rental company has just started a chauffeur service for clients

Example Three: a change of occupation from general maintenance worker to self-employed window cleaner

Strengths

1. high level of health and fitness

2. good attendance record for previous employers

3. not afraid of heights

Weaknesses

1. family are against the change

2. poor self-motivation

3. no experience of keeping financial records

Opportunities

1. an established window round is available for sale

2. reside near a heavily populated area

3. a new industrial estate has opened nearby

Threats

1. high unemployment in the area has resulted in large numbers of people working on "black economy" jobs such as window cleaning

2. unable to obtain a bank loan to buy an established window round

3. many of the homeowners prefer to clean their own windows

The examples provided should help you to conduct your own SWOT analyses. When these are complete check the results against the occupations identified and eliminate those careers that do not appear viable.

Common difficulties when considering new occupations include those of gender, age, meeting the physical requirements, lack of relevant qualifications and work experience, limited financial resources, long training periods, lack of financial assistance whilst training, lack of family support, geographical immobility, and financial restrictions such as pensions. If too many difficulties are identified it may be wise to abandon plans to pursue that occupation and focus on a career change with more chance of success.

However, not all difficulties are insurmountable and if you particularly favour a given occupation then it might be worth pursuing. There is no set rule for such a decision. As stated earlier in this chapter, it is important to remain flexible and keep a number of options open for as long as possible.

Setting realistic goals is a key factor in making a successful career change. The rest of this chapter is devoted to helping you to achieve the goals you set.

INTERNAL V EXTERNAL CAREER CHANGE

Before progressing further it is important to clarify precisely what is meant by "career change". The term "career" is often used in a general sense to describe any sequence of job changes, particularly those in middle-class occupations. The sequences involved are usually perceived as sequential and progressive – hence the term "climbing the career ladder".

Given the above view of "career" it is often difficult to distinguish between a "job" change and a "career" change. To clarify this issue it is useful to consider the five main types of employment change. These are a change of: status; industry; work activity; organization and occupation.

A CHANGE OF STATUS

This would include a change of rank within an organization (due to promotion or demotion) or a change from employee to self-employed.

A CHANGE OF INDUSTRY

In this type of change the occupation and work activity may remain the same (or change very little) but be performed within a different industrial sector. For example, an accounts clerk in the health service may move to a similar job within the chemical industry.

A CHANGE OF WORK ACTIVITY

This would involve a functional change such as a move from a managerial position in the field of marketing to a similar role within production management.

A CHANGE OF ORGANIZATION

This type of change involves a move between organizations. An example of this would be an employee of Marks & Spencer obtaining a job with British Home Stores.

A CHANGE OF OCCUPATION

This would mean a change of occupation category such as those used by Roe (1956) and Holland (1973). Examples of this would include a change from dentist to accountant, or from hairdresser to van driver.

The main focus of this book is on a change of occupation. However, many of the issues raised in relation to this are also relevant to other types of employment change and can easily be adapted for such purposes. Indeed, many changes are multi-faceted. For example, a change of occupation may also involve a change of status, organization and industry. Once a decision has been made to change occupation it is important to consider, at a very early stage, exactly what this is likely to entail. One of the first points to investigate is whether the proposed change can be accomplished within your existing organization (if employed) or if a change of organization will also be required. The opportunities for internal career change will depend largely on the occupations and the organization concerned.

The occupations: Some organizations, especially large ones, employ people from numerous occupational groups. If the occupation you wish to change to is one of those required by your current organization then an internal change of career is at least theoretically possible. For example, if a qualified engineer wished to embark on a career in management there may be opportunities to do so without a change of employer. In fact, such a change might be welcomed as a manager with practical engineering experience could prove a valuable asset to an organization. However, if the change involved a transition from marketing manager for a large firm of accountants to horticulturalist, then a change of organization would be necessary.

The organization: Organizations differ in their policies towards internal career change. Those who support such a policy do so mainly to maintain motivation and job satisfaction among employees; to prevent the loss of well-qualified, skilled and experienced employees; and to assist the organization to carry out essential restructuring. Alternatively, some organizations prefer external recruitment to take advantage of training and experience provided by other organizations; to inject "new blood" into their own organization; and to guard against any difficulties that might arise among existing staff if internal career changes are allowed.

Internal and external career change both have advantages and disadvantages for the career changer. Internal career change has the advantage of familiarity – with the organization, its policies, practices, clients and staff. On the other hand, the current organization may be the source of the career dissatisfaction, other employees may resent the changer in his new position, or it may be difficult to break away entirely from the old career. External career change offers the benefit of a completely "fresh start" in terms of the company, people and work activity. However, these should be weighed against the potential difficulties accompanying a change of employer such as relocation, pension transfers, working within an unfamiliar organizational culture, new colleagues and a possible loss of status.

A crucial aspect of the internal v external dilemma is the reason for the career change. If the proposed career change is voluntary then the above factors need to be carefully considered. However, if the change is involuntary then fewer options may be open to the changer, at least in the shorter term.

Voluntary and involuntary career change can be both internal or external in nature. In either case, research has indicated (Holmes and Cartwright, 1995) that moving towards a specified new career rather than running away from an unsatisfactory or declining current career is more desirable and has a much greater chance of success. Whatever the impetus behind your desire to change occupation, it is unwise to make hasty decisions. To reiterate earlier advice, it is important to thoroughly research several alternative careers before making a final decision.

RESEARCHING THE MARKET

As with other forms of research, "researching your market" should take the form of primary and secondary research. Primary research would involve obtaining information yourself whereas secondary research would involve making use of information collected by others. Examples of primary research would include writing to employers and to professional organizations, visiting private employment agencies and job centres and investigating training opportunities and financial assistance in relation to selected new occupations. Examples of secondary research would include studying employment trends within specified occupations and regions, reading books and articles on relevant occupations and watching appropriate television programmes on careers.

As a general rule it is best to start with secondary research. This should provide appropriate background information and help you to target areas for primary research. However, circumstances differ and you should move between the two types of research as appropriate.

Before you start any investigations it is advisable to draw up a research plan outlining: the information you need; where this can be obtained; the timescales you would like to meet and the likely costs involved. The details of a research plan depend on too many variables to be laid down specifically here. However, guidelines are proposed which should help you to develop an appropriate and useful plan within the general framework suggested.

THE INFORMATION YOU NEED

Regardless of the new career proposed it is essential to start by investigating the feasibility of such a change for you in your present circumstances. Examples of the questions you need to pose (and answer) are listed below. These are in no way exhaustive and should be added to as your research progresses.

1. Are there any restrictions limiting access to this occupation such as lower/upper age limits, height or weight requirements, specifications for sight or hearing, medical conditions which

might prevent entry?

2. What are the entry qualifications for this occupation?

   Are different pathways available for mature entrants?

   Is relevant work experience required?

   Do new entrants need to complete further training?

   Who pays for any training that is required?

   How long will any required training take?

   How will any required training be delivered?

3. What is the salary scale for this occupation?

   What are the promotion prospects?

   Are there any job perks available?

   Are there many job opportunities available?

   Is this occupation expanding or declining?

   Are job opportunities available in my region?

4. What types of jobs are available within this occupation?

   What types of work tasks would be involved in jobs?

   How varied are the work activities involved?

   How easy is it to change work activities?

   Where are jobs advertised?

   Where can I find out more about jobs in this field of work?

5. Does this occupation lend itself to self-employment?

   What aspects of the job are most suitable for this?

   Can freelance work be carried out part-time?

   How profitable is self-employment in this field?

   What type of assistance is available for self-employment?

WHERE TO OBTAIN INFORMATION

Information may be obtained from a wide variety of sources. Once again it is impossible to provide an exhaustive list but the suggestions presented here should provide a good starting point from which to build up your own data base of useful contacts. To make your research easier, the information is categorised under five headings.

Information on particular occupations:

Professional Associations and Trades Unions (e.g. the Chartered Association of Certified Accountants; the Institute of Chartered Accountants in England and Wales; the Association of Accounting Technicians; the Law Society; the Notaries Society; the British Psychological Society; the British Medical Association; the Institute of Personnel and Development and the National Union of Teachers)

Radio and television programmes on careers

Teletext information pages

Newspaper, magazine and journal articles and features

Books on careers

Talking to people already in a particular career

Local unemployment resource centres

Careers advice/guidance agencies

Information on opportunities:

Job Centres

Job Clubs and Executive Job Clubs

Private recruitment agencies

Local/national newspapers magazines

Specialist occupational journals

Specialist newspapers such as *Job and Careers* and *Jobsearch*

Notices outside organizations or on notice boards

Advance notice of jobs from people already employed by an organization

Unsolicited letters to organizations who have not advertised any jobs

Targeting organizations who are due to open up branches in your area or to expand existing branches

Regularly collate information from job adverts to find out which occupations/jobs are expanding and target your job search towards them

Information on training:

Local further education colleges

Private training agencies

Colleges of higher education

Universities

Specialist courses for adults (e.g. for Women Returners or Graduates)

Local TECs (Training and Enterprise Councils)

Evening institutes

Workers Education Association courses

Distance learning courses run by a variety of organizations (e.g. the Open University, Open College Federations, Wolsey Hall)

In-house training offered by employers

Specialist short training courses offered by organizations such as publishers, management training organizations

Specialist organizations:

Equal Opportunities Commission

Local/national associations for various disabilities

The Forties Plus Initiative (to help fight prejudice against older workers)

Specialist associations for professional and business women

Associations for ex armed services personnel

Appropriate religious organizations

Third Age First

Age Concern (England)

CAADE (The Campaign Against Age Discrimination in Employment)

METRA (The Metropolitan Authorities Recruitment Agency)

Self-employment:

Small Business Centres of banks

Local TECs

Small firms advisory agencies

"Start a Business" courses run by local further education colleges, private training agencies, correspondence schools and universities

Local chambers of commerce

The Franchise Association

THE TIMESCALES YOU WOULD LIKE TO MEET

Setting realistic goals is an essential element in researching your market. Initially, you need to draft out a plan outlining:

the information you need

where this information can be obtained

deadlines for receiving information

the time needed to process the information.

Upon completion of a research plan, you will then be in a better position to set and work towards staged goals. Experience has shown that goals are easier to achieve if they are split into smaller, more specific sub-goals. Specifying timescales for the achievement of goals and sub-goals makes it more likely that your targets will be met. However, it is important to ensure the targets set are realistic. If insufficient time is estimated, unnecessary pressure may result and you risk becoming demoralized if these self-imposed deadlines are not met. On the other hand, if too much time is allowed you may become too relaxed and complacent with the same end result – not achieving the targets set.

Effective time management is often a necessary prerequisite to setting and meeting specified targets. Drawing up a timetable of your activities over a "typical" week or month will provide useful information on the time available to carry out your market research and when this could best be carried out. Allocating specific time periods to your research may sound overly restricting but it will impose a discipline which you will find useful as your research progresses. However, timetables do not need to be adhered to rigidly; a certain amount of flexibility is essential to take account of unforseen emergencies. If these occur it is preferable to "swop" times if possible rather than reduce the amount of market research for that period.

The timescales you decide to adopt and the schedule by which you aim to achieve these will depend on the targets set and your personal and work circumstances. However, the suggestions made above should provide a useful general framework within which to plan and implement your market research.

THE LIKELY COSTS INVOLVED

Once again it is impossible to be prescriptive about these as they will depend on a number of factors including: the nature of your market research; the extent of your market research; how you collect your data; the ease with which you collect your data and the number and type of problems you encounter.

It is advisable, during your initial planning stage, to estimate the main costs likely to be involved. These will probably include postage, telephone calls, stationery, travel, purchase price of journals, newspapers, magazines, books, etc. Wherever possible reduce your costs by taking advantage of free facilities such as libraries, Job Clubs (if eligible), cheap rates, shared travel expenses, etc. However, some costs are inevitable and should be budgeted for at the outset, if possible spreading these over a number of weeks or months to lessen the impact.

At various stages throughout your market research it will be necessary to contact organizations. How you do this is an important aspect of your quest to change career.

CONTACTING ORGANIZATIONS

This apparently simple task is actually quite difficult. There is no easy formula for success but on such a well-trodden path there is a wealth of recorded experience on which to draw. Some of the most helpful suggestions have been collated and are presented here as guidelines to adapt for your own purpose. For easy reference the nucleus of this section is built around four basic questions:

which organizations to contact

why you need to contact an organization

how you can contact an organization

where organizations may be contacted

The responses given to each of these questions should form the basis of your contact plan. The more appropriate and focused your contact plan, the greater the chance of achieving your objectives.

WHICH ORGANIZATIONS TO CONTACT

The information provided in earlier sections of this chapter should be useful in helping you to answer this question. The more clearly you have identified your objectives and outlined a plan for your proposed career change, the easier it will be to identify the type(s) of organizations you need to contact. From this it should be relatively easy to draw up a list of specific organizations under each of the headings identified.

Useful sources of inspiration for this task are the various local telephone directories together with directories such as Yellow Pages, Thompsons, Business Pages, and Talking Pages. Some of these are available to all households with a telephone, others may be consulted at local libraries. Other useful source books are the more specialized business directories and reference books giving names and addresses of non-business organizations (such as educational establishments, charities, public bodies, etc.) which are available from local and central libraries.

More specialized libraries, such as those in colleges and universities, are also useful for those fortunate enough to have access to these facilities. Job Centres, Job Clubs, Careers Offices, local authorities, trades unions and professional bodies are all useful sources of information. Teletext and computer networks may also prove helpful. Often, if your initial source of contact is unable to help they can advise you where to re-direct your search.

WHY YOU NEED TO CONTACT AN ORGANIZATION

To some extent this question will have been answered when you began your search for organizations to contact. However, now that actual organizations have been identified it is time to refocus and specify precisely what it is you need from the organizations in question.

If the main purpose of your contact is to obtain general information or advice on the job market, your approach will differ to that required to obtain more detailed information on a specific occupation. In the former instance you may decide to contact a large number of organizations asking them to send you whatever information they have available; in the latter instance you need to be more precise about your requirements to help the organizations in question to meet your needs.

If you are interested in exploring the feasibility of self-employment you may require both general and specific information. For example, you may decide to contact your local TEC to find out what information is available for people in your position. Alternatively, you may wish to contact a bank to enquire about loans or other types of financial assistance for new businesses or the British Franchise Association for information on suitable franchise opportunities.

Further education and training is another area where both general and specific enquiries would be needed. Initially, you may need general information on the type of education or training courses available and where these are offered. Subsequently, you may have more specific queries such as accreditation for existing qualifications, the type of financial assistance available and alternative entry routes for mature applicants without appropriate qualifications.

The more precisely you can identify the purpose of your contact the more likely you are to obtain the information you seek with the minimum delay. It is important to remember that many of the organizations you need to contact are large and very busy. The more precise you are in your request, the easier it will be for them to help you.

HOW YOU CAN CONTACT AN ORGANIZATION

The main options open to you are contact by letter, telephone and personal visit. In many instances it is appropriate (and necessary) to use two or all three of these options. For example, initial contact may be by letter with a follow up telephone call or a personal visit. Alternatively, the initial contact may be telephone or personal visit followed up by a letter. There is no simple rule on which option(s) to use. This will usually depend on the circumstances (such as the nature and proximity of the contact) and the contactee (such as their boldness, sense of urgency and determination).

The choice of option(s) will also depend on whether or not the contact is solicited or unsolicited. Unsolicited contact occurs when contact has not been invited. Examples of unsolicited contact including writing to a number of organizations enquiring about job vacancies; calling in at a Job Centre to discuss job or training opportunities; telephoning a college to enquire about courses or asking to see the manager of a local supermarket to ask if they need cashiers. Solicited contact occurs when contact has been invited. Examples of solicited contact include writing in response to a job advertisement in the local newspaper; calling to see the manager of a shop in response to a notice in their window; telephoning the Job Centre in response to a radio announcement that temporary clerical work was available in your area; or ringing a local company that had advertised job vacancies on teletext.

When contacting an organization, it is always useful to target your enquiry at a particular person. If the contact is unsolicited you should try to obtain the name of an appropriate person prior to making contact. This can usually be obtained by ringing up an organization in advance and asking who is responsible for a particular job function (such as "head of personnel", "head of engineering" or "sales manager"). If the contact is solicited then a contact name is usually quoted as part of an advertisement.

To increase the chance of response to unsolicited letters, it is useful to include a stamped addressed envelope for the reply. In the case of solicited contacts it is important to note if a stamped addressed envelope is required. If it is and you do not notice this request, you may not receive a reply.

If the contact is unsolicited, how you make contact is left to your own preference. However, since organizations receive many unsolicited letters and CVs, the most productive approach may be to send a brief letter stating the type of job you would like information about, what you have to offer and the likelihood of future vacancies in this area. If the contact is solicited it is important to obey the instructions given. For example, if you are asked to "write in" or "telephone" then do so. Ignoring the instructions for contact in such instances may antagonize the organization concerned and jeopardize your chance of gaining a job or training place.

Three important documents are likely to be involved at some stage of your attempts to secure a job or a place on an education or training course. These are a curriculum vitae, a letter of application and an application form.

A curriculum vitae is vitally important as a marketing tool in securing job-related interviews or making speculative contacts with organizations. In themselves they do not get jobs – people get jobs not CVs. The preparation of CVs and what should go into them is a controversial area; different people have different ideas. Fashions in CV writing do change. The increasing number of professional CV writing agencies has led to the development of extremely lengthy portfolios which often include photographs of the applicant. The problem with CVs which are prepared by external agencies is that they are often inflexible – one comprehensive document is prepared to "fit" all situations. An individual, with access to modern personal computer packages, should be able to produce a CV of high quality, which can be tailored to meet specific situations.

As well as standard personal biographical information, the CV should include:

work experience, beginning with most recent employment

a summary of educational qualifications, aptitudes, professional or trade associations and interests

a statement of achievements, both work and non-work related.

In the USA, it is illegal for employers to ask age-related questions on application forms or at interviews. If you consider that disclosing your age may jeopardize your chances, do not include it unless specifically directed to do so.

In the past, it was a convention to prepare a CV in a strictly chronological format. In recognition that the primary objective of the CV is to capture the interest of its recipient, more distinctive and dynamic alternative forms of CV have become recognized as being more effective. Those which provide a powerful up-front section which briefly summarizes experiences and achievements, and gives a kind of 20 to 30 second commercial or postcard size advertisement of yourself can be particularly effective. An example of such a CV is shown in Figure 2.1

Again, there are a number of publications which provide useful guidance on preparing a CV. For example, *Super Job Search* by Peter Studner (1989) is an excellent source for professionals and managers. Cartwright and Cooper (1994) give a few basic tips.

A CV should not be too long – ideally no more than three pages.

It should be typewritten or handwritten in black pen, so that it can easily be photocopied by potential employers. This also applies to covering letters and application forms.

Use short and punchy sentences.

Experiment with layout, headings, margins, coloured paper, etc. to make it distinctive.

Say more about your recent work experiences and less the further back in the past you go.

Always enclose with a covering letter. Putting your CV into a folder or clear perspex sleeve is also a good idea. It will ensure that it remains in the pristine condition it was when it left your possession, and will prevent it from incurring accidental damage, coffee spills, etc. which may unfairly detract from its appearance.

It is important to inform the people whose names you may have given as references on application forms and provide them with a copy of your CV, together with some background details regarding any application so that they can focus their comments. Similarly, if you are responding to a job advertisement, try to incorporate some of the key words contained in the advert into your covering letter.

WHERE ORGANIZATIONS MAY BE CONTACTED

Once again, the nature of the contact is important. For unsolicited contact you will need to make use of personal knowledge or appropriate

CURRICULUM VITAE

Robert Smith   Telephone: **0283 7546**
4 Clare Court
Ashby
Middlesex A14 2BY

Twelve years experience dealing with the general public as a betting shop manager. Extensive cash handling, sales promotions and general management experience.

* **Increased turnover of unit by 100% over 3 years**
* **Highly numerate with a mature and methodical approach**
* **Assisted with a company takeover in London**

A sensible and reliable person who has a proven record of loyalty and commitment seeking the opportunity to build on and widen their managerial experience.

ACHIEVEMENTS

* **Developed a training programme for cashiers and managers**
* **Supervised staff of all ages**
* **Progressed to manager of a high turnover unit and maintained that role for five years**

EXPERIENCE

Arrow Racing Limited   **1983 - 1995**
Ashby

Betting Shop Manager

Manager for various units in the area. Five years at Ashby unit - turnover £1.5 million. Directly supervised four staff.

Reason for leaving : greater managerial challenge

Forrest Green Post Office   **1981 - 1983**
Dean Valley

Counter Clerk

Responsible for serving the public in this busy local office. Managed the office in the owners' absence and was responsible for producing the weekly returns.

Reason for leaving : to further ambitions

48

EDUCATION

- 5 'O' Levels - Mathematics, Advanced Mathematics, English Language Geography and Physics

- 2 'A' Levels - Pure Maths and Applied Maths

- HND (Business Studies) - Fairfield College of Education - 1979-1981

- Short management courses in constructive negotiation, effective speaking and human relations

INTERESTS

Reading, football and table tennis.

CAREER AMBITIONS

I want to secure employment within an environment that will enable me to further develop my managerial skills and gain insight into a different business sector/industry. I am single and willing to re-locate, if necessary.

reference sources (such as directories, teletext, Yellow Pages, etc.) to find out the address of the organization you need to contact. If it is a national organization you need to decide at which level initial contact is most appropriate. For example, if you are enquiring about entry qualifications for a profession then you may decide to contact the head office. Alternatively, if you are enquiring about job vacancies it is usually more appropriate to write to your nearest shop or branch. Solicited contacts should be directed at the contact address or telephone number provided. In some instances you may only have access to a local address. This may be used as an initial point of contact. If the local branch is unable to help you they can then provide the address of their regional or national office. The names and addresses of organizations likely to be of general use to career changers are provided in the appendices.

Effective networking

Establishing and developing a network of formal and informal contacts should be a crucial element in any career change strategy. For example, nearly 70% of managerial jobs are never advertised. The cliché "it's not *what* you know but *who* you know" is so over-used people often say it without really focusing on its meaning. The phrase is often used in a derogatory sense to explain or excuse our own lack of success. However, if viewed in a more positive light it can also be the key to success for its critics.

A common complaint in relation to networking is: "I don't have a network!" This is clearly untrue; everyone has a network. In fact, to be more precise, they usually have a series of networks. What they usually lack is an appreciation of what a "network" is and how it can best be used to their advantage. The aim of this section is to help readers benefit from the networks to which they already have access, and to develop new networks appropriate to their current needs.

Formal and informal networks

Although there is often considerable overlap between these two types of network it is useful to distinguish between them from the outset. A "formal" network is one established for the purpose of providing contact between like-minded individuals who share a particular kind of interest (such as business, charitable, political, social, sporting, religious, etc.). Formal networks would include professional associations, trades unions, football supporters' clubs, swimming clubs, political parties, and trades associations. The structure of these organizations, their relationship with members, and their links with other similar organizations at home and abroad provide useful contacts for members.

An "informal" network consists of people with whom you come into contact in a variety of capacities who may also provide useful advice, information, and support for various areas of your life if needed. Informal networks range from family and friends, to work colleagues and casual acquaintances, clients and business associates.

The purpose of networks

A common response when asked "what is the purpose of networking?" is that networks provide useful contacts to help *you* achieve your goals. In a sense this is true. However, if all network members have this as their sole or prime objective, then the system would soon collapse.

The key principle in respect to networking is reciprocity: the sharing of information together with mutual advice and support between network members. This principle should apply to both formal and informal networks. Anyone who tries to consistently "take" from other network members without being willing (or able) to "give" anything in return is a weak link in the chain and unlikely to be tolerated by other members indefinitely.

Networks may best be viewed as a collection of people whose individual knowledge, skills, experience and contacts are limited but when combined together can provide a much stronger database from which members can draw.

Effective networking

This may be divided into three stages.

Stage One: identifying existing networks. This is important for everyone but particularly for those who claim not to have any "networks". A simple but effective way to do this is to think of the type of people with whom you have regular contact (such as family, friends, colleagues at work, neighbours, postman, golfing partners, shop assistants, garage mechanics, doctors, dentists, etc.), and write a detailed list of these.

When you have exhausted your list of contacts, go through the list and classify then into groups – for example, family, friends, casual acquaintances, trade acquaintances, work colleagues, competitors, clients, sporting enthusiasts, etc. When everyone on your list has been classified, go through each heading again and see if you can add anyone else to your list for that category. It is surprising how the use of categories triggers off the memory. The purpose of this task is twofold: to identify the different types of networks to which you already have access and to identify people who belong to the networks identified.

Stage Two: developing existing networks. Once you have identified existing networks it is important to activate them (if you have not previously thought of or used them as networks) or develop them if your current networks have not been fully utilized.

In the case of formal networks this might mean attending more meetings, renewing membership subscriptions, attending more social functions, or generally renewing or enhancing business acquaintances. In the case of informal networks this might mean talking more to neighbours and tradespeople, socialising more with friends and relatives, or renewing or increasing your interest in a sport or hobby. In all cases you should adopt a subtle approach as people generally resent being "used". In addition, remember that networking applies equally to all parties; if you want something from someone you must be prepared to offer something in return.

Stage Three: establishing new networks. This stage of networking provides the most scope for focusing on the type of contacts that will prove of most use in your search for a new career. In some instances, this would include informal contact with course tutors, fellow students, business colleagues and acquaintances. In addition, you might decide to join new professional associations which you feel would increase your chances of success, or take up a new sport or hobby which would provide useful contacts.

This type of networking requires a conscious effort to seek out people and groups who can help you during the various stages of your proposed career change. In the early stages this may mean providing valuable insight into occupations that are of interest to you or providing useful advice and guidance on how to enter a new occupation. During the transitional period this may take the form of assistance with training, advice on where to obtain finance, help with finding placements or temporary work. In the final stages this may involve introductions to prospective employers, advice on how to gain access to jobs within a new occupational field, advance warning on new posts within organizations, or introductions to prospective clients if you decide to become self-employed.

SPECIALIST NETWORKING

The networking discussed so far is fairly general and would be applicable to most people and situations. For many people this type of networking is sufficient. However, others may also require more specialist networks if they are to succeed. These "specialist networks" may take various forms, for example, networks for women, ethnic groups, or people with disabilities. Fortunately, because it is widely recognized that some people in these categories may need additional help and support, facilities are now available to meet their needs. Information on such networks is available from telephone directories, local libraries, further education colleges, Job Centres, careers advisory services and local authorities.

One group of people who are also likely to need specialist networks but whose needs have been largely ignored are "older workers". The ageing nature of the population and workforce in the United Kingdom means membership of this "group" is increasing. Currently, one-third of the population is aged 45 or over. Unfortunately, older workers are a popular and easy target for employers wishing to rationalize their workforce and, once unemployed, they find it more difficult than those in younger age groups to regain employment (*Social Trends* 1990 and 1991). This is due to two main factors: age discrimination is not illegal in the United Kingdom and employers generally have a negative image of older workers.

Some professional associations and trades unions have taken the initiative in condemning age discrimination by employers, and some employers, including the government itself, actively seek to employ older workers. The government has also recently launched a series of initiatives (such as an Advisory Group on Older Workers) to help reverse the trend.

Anyone who falls within the category of "older worker" may thus find it more difficult than younger workers to change occupation. Identifying organizations who include age as part of their equal opportunities policy or who actively recruit older applicants is an important aspect of networking for this age group.

A number of local, regional and national initiatives have also been set up to help older workers combat against discrimination by employers. Membership of such organisations is another form of specialist networking. Details of some of the more widely publicised initiatives are included in the appendices.

With practice, effective networking should become both automatic and continuous. There is no limit to networking. For continued effectiveness, networks need to be perpetually monitored, reappraised, revised and added to as required. Networking also needs to become so automatic that we do it without thinking – alert to opportunities whenever they present themselves. In addition, it is sometimes necessary to seek out opportunities rather than wait for them to present themselves.

Sources of career advice and guidance

There are numerous formal sources of advice and guidance, other than Job Centres and Job Clubs. All large towns and cities have a Careers Service Office which can be a useful source of information on jobs, training, university courses, etc. Many provide specific adult guidance services. University careers advisory services provide a free facility for current and past students. Local libraries are also potential sources of career information. Many institutions of higher and further education run short courses which could be useful to the unemployed or women returners in the areas of skill training or those considering starting up a new business. Help in this area is also available from local enterprise agencies, the Training and Enterprise Council (TEC) or the small business centres of banks.

There are a number of private consultancy practices which offer careers guidance for a fee. These are usually run by or employ the services of an occupational psychologist. Typically, the assessment and consultation processes involve in-depth interviews and the completion of a series of psychometric tests and questionnaires to ascertain individual aptitudes and suitability for certain kinds of work or training. As well as advising on potential career paths, many outplacement organizations also provide advice and skill training on CV preparation, interview techniques, etc.

Self-help manuals such as *Build Your Own Rainbow* (Hopson and Scally, 1984) and *What Color is Your Parachute?* (Nelson-Bolles, 1989) can be useful in helping the individual identify career possibilities. The Open University produces a relatively inexpensive self-development pack comprising workbooks, self-assessment questionnaires, etc., designed to help the individual to realize his or her potential.

When consulting any source of careers advice and guidance it is important to remember that their role is to: provide appropriate careers information; refer you to other, more specialist, sources of advice and guidance if required and help you to evaluate the career options available to you. It is not part of their job to make decisions on career change: the only person who can do that is *you*. It is your responsibility (to yourself and relevant others) to put yourself in the position where you can make informed decisions.

At this stage of the career-change process you may feel confused about the amount and complexity of information at your disposal, daunted by the amount of work involved and anxious about making the "right" decision. It is thus an appropriate time to introduce the concept of "modelling".

It is unlikely that earlier career changers will have identical qualifications, experience, skills and circumstances to you. However, their career change experiences (successful and unsuccessful) should provide useful models for people who have embarked (or are about to embark) on a change of occupation themselves. Chapter three presents a number of these models and provides the opportunity for you to learn from their experiences.

CHAPTER THREE

LEARNING FROM OTHERS

Each career change experience is unique but learning from others can be a useful short-cut to success. In recognition of this, case studies of successful and unsuccessful career changers are presented in this chapter to provide readers with examples of what to follow or avoid in their own attempts to change occupation.

Before focusing on specific examples of career change, the chapter summarises findings from relevant research into career change by considering popular motives for change, the factors most likely to facilitate and hinder change, and general expectations relating to new careers. In addition, key factors associated with a successful career change are identified and discussed.

To accomplish these tasks the chapter is divided into four sections:

Career changers: their motives, problems and expectations

Career change: key factors

Case studies of successful career changers

Case studies of unsuccessful career changers

Although this chapter adopts a generally narrative style, it is important for readers to become actively involved by continually visualizing themselves in the positions reported. By identifying similarities and differences with their own position, readers should be able to discover what would or would not work for them.

CAREER CHANGERS: THEIR MOTIVES, PROBLEMS AND EXPECTATIONS

Investigations into career change have focused on key issues such as motives for change, factors most likely to help or hinder change and expectations of new careers. Patterns have emerged that point to fundamental differences between career changers and non-changers that cut across situational factors (Holmes and Cartwright, 1994). A brief consideration of these patterns is a useful way to start learning from others.

MOTIVES

Individuals change jobs or careers for a variety of reasons. The first thing to consider is whether the change is voluntary or involuntary in nature. To some extent, all career change is voluntary, even that prompted by changing employment trends. A shrinking job market in one occupation may signal the need to seek a new career but this does not guarantee change or specify the direction such change should take.

Research findings indicate that career change is most likely to occur among people who:

are concerned about the quality of life and feel their present career is not sufficiently satisfying or fulfilling;

are suffering from a mid-career crisis;

have a personality profile which indicates high levels of energy, independence, creativity and adaptability;

have a strong need for achievement and intellectual stimulation;

require a high level of variety in their job;

require a new challenge;

want to make full use of their experience and skills.

These motives are quite diverse but all indicate needs that emanate from within the individual.

People who do not change careers may have similar needs to those outlined for career changers, but these are often weaker than their external needs. In such cases, work motivation may be more strongly influenced by the need for:

job security;

financial rewards;

opportunities for promotion;

job status;

a pleasant physical environment;

cordial colleagues;

appreciative employers.

In many instances, a change of career may not be necessary to satisfy these types of needs, which could be satisfied by a change in employer.

It is important to continually and honestly examine your own motives for a change of occupation. Is it the type of work that you do which causes your discontent, or the work environment or organization in which you do it? If, after searching examination, you decide your needs can no longer be satisfied within your existing occupation, then a change of career is indicated. However, it may be that the sources of dissatisfaction lie with your current work duties, in which case a change of function would suffice. Alternatively, the dissatisfaction may be traced to conflict within your organization (with colleagues or managers) and a change of employer is necessary.

Although it is impossible to generalize, motivation to change career is often related to age. The is due to either poor initial career choice or (more often) to changing attitudes and values. When younger workers decide to change career it is mainly to satisfy their external needs for greater financial rewards, better career prospects, or more varied work experience. Older workers are generally more concerned with satisfying their internal needs for skill utilization, goal achievement and job fulfilment, although they are also concerned with job stability and security.

Mid-career is a particularly traumatic time for many workers. It is a time for career reappraisal which often results in disillusionment relating to unfulfilled goals, perceived lack of appreciation, reduced motivation and the desire for a new challenge. Linked to the aspects of motivation discussed earlier such reflection may result in a radical career move. Alternatively, personality and/or circumstances may work against a job or career change at this time. This may result in a further decline in motivation and reduced loyalty to employers. In many cases, this is only temporary and non-changers become more resigned and accepting of their position.

PROBLEMS

Radical career change is relatively rare. This is not surprising given the number of difficulties associated with a change of occupation. The main obstacles to career change include:

a lack of relevant experience, qualifications and skills;

ageism by employers;

lack of job opportunities;

family responsibilities;

financial restrictions (such as rigid pension schemes);

personal limitations;

fear of change;

lack of training facilities and financial assistance;

inadequate careers advice and guidance.

The extent of these problems varies with individuals, as does their ability to overcome them. The main facilitators of career change include:

personal motivation;

job opportunities;

family support;

adequate education/training provision;

perceptive/appreciative employers;

relevant experience, qualifications and skills;

personal characteristics;

an improving economy.

The self-knowledge and knowledge of the market gained from the two previous chapters should act as good provisional indicators of the type of difficulties you would face if you decided to change occupation and your ability to overcome these difficulties. If you feel daunted by the prospect of changing career and overwhelmed by the perceived difficulties then perhaps you should seriously reconsider your decision to change. On the other hand, if you acknowledge the difficulties but see them as obstacles to overcome and are confident of your ability to do so, then you should be well-equipped to pursue your plans to change career.

EXPECTATIONS

When considering a change of career, it is important to consider not only why you wish to leave your current occupation but also what attracts you to alternative occupations. In chapter one you were asked to consider what you liked most and least about your current (or last) job or career. It is advisable to reflect on your response before proceeding further with this section.

What employees like and dislike about a job or career affects both why they leave and what they expect from any change they may make. Research indicates that, generally, employees like jobs that require their active involvement, have variety of tasks, are stimulating, meaningful, offer opportunities for career development and bestow dignity on the jobholder. They usually dislike jobs that are monotonous, repetitive, over-controlled and lack opportunities for social interaction.

Our own investigations have shown that to be considered successful a career change should:

enhance health, happiness and peace of mind;

lead to an improved personal life;

provide opportunities for full skill utilization;

provide greater opportunities for responsibility;

provide greater job/business opportunities;

lead to a sense of achievement;

increase job satisfaction/fulfilment;

provide improved financial security;

improve job security;

reduce travel commitments.

Of course, the extent to which these outcomes are considered important will vary with individuals. In addition, the list itself is by no means exhaustive but reflects the views of a research sample of managers and professionals. Readers should use the list to identify which of the outcomes presented are important to them. Any additional outcomes can then be added to the list.

Once complete, the lists can be used to determine the extent to which any proposed career change would satisfy your specified outcomes. It is unlikely that any one career would fulfil all your requirements. However, the more a new occupation appears to meet your expectations the more confidence you will have to pursue it. Conversely, if the proposed career change is unlikely to meet your expectations, it is unwise to pursue it further and an alternative occupation should be sought.

CAREER CHANGE: KEY FACTORS

The key factors discussed in this section are based on the findings of a recent study of mid-career change amongst managers and professionals aged 35+. This involved the collection of qualitative (interview) and quantitative (questionnaire) data. The research explored the differences between over 300 successful and unsuccessful career changers. Although targeted at a specific group of career changers, the findings provide a useful basis from which to consider change among other occupational groups.

The authors do not claim the findings present a "blueprint" for successful career change. However, they do indicate important personal and situational differences between successful and unsuccessful career changers which should prove useful to others about to embark on a change themselves. The findings are presented under three main headings: age; job/career mobility and locus of control.

AGE

As anticipated, age did emerge as a major barrier to mid-career change. However, significant differences were noted between successful and unsuccessful career changers in their attitude towards age. Individuals with a history of successful job and career change placed less emphasis on age as an obstacle to change than those who had been unsuccessful in their attempts to change career. This was apparent from responses to rating scales, open questions on barriers to career change and comments made in letters or telephone calls.

Other factors such as the extent and pattern of job or career mobility, direction of change, motives and expectations were found to cut across age groups. It is these "other factors" that explained why people with similar qualifications, work experience, age, and aspirations fared differently in their attempts to change occupation.

Mid-career was also confirmed as a time for major career reappraisal. Findings suggest that the main reasons for reassessment at this time include necessity, the need for increased security and financial rewards, the need for a new challenge, increased job satisfaction and a more meaningful job. In addition, a desire for change was often prompted by structural changes within organizations and negative perceptions of an employee's role within an organization.

JOB/CAREER MOBILITY

As anticipated, different patterns of job and career mobility were noted between successful and unsuccessful career changers. Successful career changers emerged as considerably more mobile than their less successful counterparts. Findings suggest the existence of a group of managers and professionals who pursue a career change at regular intervals. Among successful career changers 93.2% had changed career between 1 and 5 times compared with 56.4% of the unsuccessful group; and 43.8% of the unsuccessful group had failed in all their career change attempts.

The evidence suggests that "success" can be self-perpetuating, with successful career changers having the confidence, experience and motivation to make further changes. Conversely, when job and career change attempts are unsuccessful, confidence is reduced, which often discourages further attempts to change occupation.

A further important difference between successful and unsuccessful career changers is that the former generally moved towards a specified new career whereas the latter often attempted to drift away from an existing career. This lack of direction among unsuccessful career changers was a major factor in their lack of success.

LOCUS OF CONTROL

As anticipated, findings indicated that successful career changers had a significantly higher internal locus of control than unsuccessful changers. This means they believed a successful career change was within their own control and personal influence. The higher levels of external locus of control displayed by the unsuccessful group reflected their belief that a successful career change was largely determined by other (external) forces beyond their control.

The internal/external nature of respondents' locus of control was revealed by responses to the ratings scales and the open questions relating to motives, obstacles and expectations. On each of the four ratings scales completed as part of the research (motives, facilitatory/ inhibitory, spector locus of control and outcomes) members of the unsuccessful group (on average) revealed a higher external locus of control than members of the successful group. When responses to open-ended questions were analysed both groups gave a high priority to internal motives (such as job satisfaction and the need for a new challenge) and outcomes (such as increased job satisfaction) although the unsuccessful group emphasized external factors (such as promotion prospects, financial rewards, and job security) more than the successful group.

The main differences between the two groups was found in their attitude to the barriers or obstacles to career change they encountered. Successful career changers placed far less emphasis on external obstacles to change (such as lack of support, advice and guidance and the negative attitude of employers) and pursued their career change with greater determination.

Differences between successful and unsuccessful career changers were particularly apparent from an analysis of their initial letters and contents of telephone conversations. Successful career changers consistently demonstrated a more positive attitude and pursued their change with greater determination than unsuccessful changers. Unsuccessful changers also placed more emphasis on external obstacles and were more inclined to blame other people and circumstances for their lack of success.

REVIEW OF KEY POINTS

The research findings outlined in this section highlight the main differences between successful and unsuccessful career changers in the sample studied. A brief summary of the key points identified are presented overleaf for easy reference.

Age is, potentially a major obstacle to mid-career change but can be overcome.

Successful career changers are generally more mobile than those who have been unsuccessful in their attempts to change career.

A pattern of "multiple careers' was identified among some successful career changers pointing to a core of "perpetual" career changers.

Successful career changers were far more likely to focus on a specified new occupation whereas unsuccessful changers often tried to move away from an unsatisfactory existing career.

Successful career changers were significantly more internally motivated and controlled than unsuccessful career changers.

Successful career changers had significantly more positive attitudes towards career change than unsuccessful changers; they were far more prepared to create and exploit opportunities for career change and to accept responsibility for any problems they encountered.

To summarise the main differences between successful and unsuccessful career changers: successful career changers placed a greater emphasis on controlling their own careers and were thus better able to overcome obstacles to change such as ageism and a weak economy; unsuccessful career changers, with their greater emphasis on external influences, were less able to overcome these obstacles and were consequently less successful in their attempts to change career.

The main aim of this section is to help readers recognize the important role played by personal characteristics in achieving a successful career change. It is not meant to encourage either over-complacency in some or despair in others. The recognition of potential weaknesses is the first step to overcoming them.

To benefit most from this section it is important to identify which of the research findings presented apply to you. Unfortunately, we do not always possess the self-knowledge or the honesty required to conduct such a candid self-appraisal. In view of this, it is always useful to seek other people's opinions. However, you need to be selective about the people you choose for this task. For the exercise to be productive the people chosen must be those who know you well, are prepared to give an honest assessment of your personal characteristics and express views that you are likely to value and accept.

The models of successful and unsuccessful career changers presented should help you to identify the main ingredients required to make a successful career change and help you to determine your main weaknesses in relation to the model of successful career changer. Once potential weaknesses have been recognized you have three options available.

Accept these weaknesses and decide you still wish to pursue your chosen career change. If you select this option then you need to incorporate these weaknesses into your plans and devise strategies to help you overcome them.

Postpone your plans to change career until you feel more confident about success and until you have time to spend on correcting your weaknesses. If you select this option, it is still worthwhile working through the remaining chapters of the book to help you plan your future career change.

Abandon your plans to change career. If you select this option it could indicate a lack of real commitment to your alternative occupation, a lack of necessity for the change or a lack of determination to pursue a career change in the face of perceived threats to the success of your venture. In this case although you may decide not to finish reading the book, you have clearly benefited from what you have read so far. You have not failed in your task: you have sensibly decided a career change is either not necessary or not important enough for you to pursue. The self-knowledge required for making such a decision will benefit you in the future and you may have saved yourself from wasting time and energy pursuing a career change that would not have been successful.

The importance of learning from others should now be apparent. So far, the learning involved has been from general models based on various investigations into career change. The remaining sections of this chapter focus on specific examples of career change (successful and unsuccessful attempts) that emerged from one of these investigations.

CASE STUDIES OF SUCCESSFUL CAREER CHANGERS

The case studies presented in this section have been selected for their diversity. Table I gives brief details of the types of career change which were successfully made by a sample of participants taken from the study.

Although the career changes quoted had been made for a wide variety of reasons, the majority of changes were in response to "internal needs" such as increased job satisfaction, the desire for a change, or for a more interesting career. The more "external" motives such as redundancy, business failure or family circumstances often hide the fact that a new career was deliberately sought.

Some of the new careers mainly involved changes of function or status (for example different types of manager or from employee to self-employed). However, some were quite radical in nature (for example retailer to teacher; chef to antique dealer). Many of these changes were carefully planned, often involving quite lengthy retraining periods.

Five of these case studies are now discussed in more detail to further illustrate the motives that prompted the change; the factors that most helped and hindered the change; the main difficulties encountered; the expectations for the change and the desire (or intention) to make further career changes.

CASE STUDY NO. 1

John Davis had been involved in the printing trade since he left school at 15. He had started as an office junior and gradually worked his way up to become sales manager. During his long career in printing he had worked for three employers and was very happy and satisfied with his career.

In March 1989, his company was taken over by a larger company and a process of "rationalization" took place which resulted in John being made redundant after 25 years' uninterrupted service. At the age of 52 John realised it would be difficult to find another job of comparable pay and status. He decided this was the ideal opportunity to change career and pursue a secret ambition: to become a full-time writer.

TABLE 1   EXAMPLES OF SUCCESSFUL CAREER CHANGERS

Gender	Age at Change	Changed From	Changed To	Reasons for Change
Male	35	Army Officer	Sales Representative	End of army contract
Male	38	Boilermaker	Full time student	Redundancy
Male	43	Catering Manager	Chef	Desire for change
Male	52	Chef	Antique dealer	Redundancy/interest
Female	49	Civil servant	Freelance computer analyst	Redundancy
Female	52	College Lecturer	Training advisor	Early retirement
Male	43	Computer analyst	Marketing manager	Lack of interest
Female	54	Computer analyst	Computer software manufacturer	Job satisfaction
Female	38	Computer analyst	Accountant	Job satisfaction
Male	53	Financial advisor	Practice manager	Early retirement
Male	43	Hotel owner	Training consultant	Desire for change
Female	42	Legal executive	Freelance legal work	Job satisfaction
Male	50	Marketing manager	Management consultant	Desire for change
Male	40	Commercial manager	English as a foreign language (overseas) EFL Teacher	Redundancy
Male	55	Management consultant	Careers consultant	Desire for change
Male	50	Marketing manager	Financial advisor	Desire for change
Female	28	Manager	Retail shop owner	Interest
Female	45	Nurse	Writer	Family situation/interest
Female	35	Personnel Officer	Training advisor	Job satisfaction
Male	30	Retail shop owner	Maths teacher	Job satisfaction
Male	61	Restaurant owner	Employment Agency owner	Desire for change
Female	59	Software manufacturer	Technical Author	Desire for change
Male	38	Teacher	Financial advisor	More freedom
Male	50	Training consultant	Restaurant owner	Lack of business

John had always written as a hobby, was a member of his local writers' club and had managed to get a number of letters, "fillers" and even some short stories published. He realized it would be difficult, especially at first, but there were a number of factors in his favour: his redundancy money would provide a financial buffer; his children were grown-up, married and financially independent; his wife still worked and fully supported his plans and he had repaid his mortgage.

Initially, there was (as anticipated) quite a substantial drop in income. However, the increased satisfaction and sense of accomplishment more than compensated for this. Three years later John is beginning to reap the benefits of his new occupation and has no regrets. His advice to anyone else in a similar position is "go for it" – but only if the circumstances are right and you have the self-belief and confidence to succeed.

CASE STUDY NO. 2

Carole Miller left school at 18 after gaining 3 "A" levels (in Mathematics, Physics and Chemistry) and obtained employment as a laboratory technician in a large pharmaceutical company. The company encouraged her to embark on further studies and supported her financially while she completed an HNC (part-time) at her local polytechnic. Carole married at 24 and moved from the south east to the north west of England. She managed to obtain a similar job where she stayed for three years before deciding to take a five year career break when her two children were born.

When she returned to work (aged 32) she no longer found the work satisfying but her family commitments made it difficult for her to retrain for a new career. To help her overcome increasing dissatisfaction with her job, Carole took a number of part-time courses which qualified her as a fitness trainer. She managed to supplement her income by holding part-time fitness classes in local church halls and community centres.

The opportunity to change career came at the age of 37 when her company announced large reductions in staffing levels and invited applications for voluntary redundancy. It was a difficult decision to make. She had a young family, a mortgage and her husband's job was not very secure. After much contemplation Carole decided to take the voluntary redundancy and become a self-employed personal fitness trainer/instructor.

The main problems she encountered were financial (at first) and combining running a business with her heavy family commitments. However, hard work and determination brought success within the first twelve months. Carole now earns more money in a day than she earned in a week in her previous career. More importantly, the job satisfaction is much greater, and she has far more personal and professional freedom.

Carole has plans to expand her business within the next two years by diversifying into other related areas, such as massage and aromatherapy. She also hopes to employ staff to help her with the expansion.

Carole's advice to others in a similar position is to think very carefully before making a decision. She feels you need to be very confident and dedicated to succeed in self-employment. Also, if you have family commitments you need their full support. She herself has no regrets about changing career but feels her previous experience of operating the business on a part-time basis first was the sensible approach and would advise others to follow her example in this respect to discover if they enjoy the job and if it is financially viable.

CASE STUDY NO. 3

David Fletcher has accomplished two career changes, one quite radical in nature. He had always been interested in music and became a professional musician upon leaving school at 17. He thoroughly enjoyed his job although he never earned very much money. In the early days he particularly liked the travelling. By his early twenties, David began to tire of the travelling and insecurity and decided to change career. However, he was reluctant to leave the music business entirely and decided to train as a music technician.

This first career change was completed at the age of 25 when David moved to London and worked as a technician for a number of record companies. He enjoyed his new career and did not consider a further career change until his late thirties when he began to feel the need for a more worthwhile job. After considering a number of options he decided to retrain as a social worker and obtained his first full-time job in this field at the age of 44.

This second, radical career change was mainly prompted by the desire for increased job satisfaction (perhaps by helping others); a desire to leave London; the lack of job opportunities in his current area of work and the desire for a new challenge.

He chose social work because job opportunities could occur across the country, because it satisfied his need to help others and because mature applicants were accepted. Before making a final decision he participated in a variety of voluntary social work projects to make sure he would enjoy the work. The main problems he encountered related to the long training period involved, adjusting to life as a mature student and the initial drop in pay whilst training.

David does not regret his decision and feels that, in the long term, he will have more job security and greater job satisfaction. His advice to others who may be considering a mid-career change is: research your options carefully; make sure you have the support of your family; consider the long-term prospects of any potential new career; talk to as many people as possible to find out what a proposed new career entails and try to experience the new career (e.g. on a part-time or voluntary basis) before making a final decision.

CASE STUDY NO. 4

Moira Bates left school at 18 having gained three "A" levels in History, English and Geography. She accepted a place at a teacher training college and taught primary school children in a number of schools, eventually gaining a position as deputy headmistress at the age of 38.

During her early forties she began to reassess her career. She realized she no longer wanted to become head of school but had no clear idea of an alternative career. However, she had always been very active in church affairs and had been a lay preacher for ten years. Her husband was also very involved in the church and both her teenage children were regular churchgoers.

Moira cannot recall making a definite decision to change career, but gradually moved in a new direction until it became a logical move to leave teaching and work full-time for the church. Upon reflection the change was motivated by a strong sense of "vocation" which gradually moved her towards her new career as church minister. She was 48 when she obtained her first full-time appointment but her many years of work in voluntary capacity provided excellent preparation for her new role.

Despite the gradual change and strong desire to follow her vocational urgings, Moira was still apprehensive about her new career. Fear of the unknown and uncertainty about the exact nature of the job and her ability to perform her duties well were the main problems encountered. The drop in income was not seen as a problem and she had the full support of her family. Moira also experienced much greater job satisfaction and sense of fulfilment in her new role and has no plans to make any further career change.

Although her career change appears radical, Moira feels the slow, gradual transition protected her from the full impact of the change. Her advice to others is to follow their instincts and not be too concerned about financial rewards or status, or the opinion of others. This does not include close family members, since such a momentous decision needs their help and support.

Planning is also seen as very important and, wherever possible, experiencing a new role prior to making any definite commitment. This is particularly important if retraining is required. Age should not be seen as a barrier to change, particularly if past knowledge and experiences are relevant to the new career.

CASE STUDY NO. 5

Thomas Stones joined the army at 21 after graduating with a degree in engineering. His army career was varied and he rose to the rank of major. Although he had always enjoyed his army career Thomas was keen to prepare for civilian life and took a number of correspondence courses, mainly in the areas of training and management.

It was shortly after his fortieth birthday that Thomas began to reassess his life and career. It had been an eventful year which culminated in divorce and he began to think seriously about a radical career change. At the age of 45 he left the army and gained employment as training advisor for a large chemical company. He found his new post interesting at first but soon realized he needed something more challenging.

After three years, aged 48, he then obtained a job as security advisor where he could make better use of his army training and experience. This job was more satisfying but after a while it too became restricting. He remained in this job for two years then left, at the age of 50, to set up his own security company. This proved very successful and for the next ten years the business continued to expand to include lucrative home and overseas security consultancy contracts. At the age of 60 Thomas decided to sell the company and retire. However, he soon became bored with retirement and accepted a position as operations manager with a large manufacturing company.

The main motivation for career change was always the desire for a new challenge, which usually included travel and excitement. Thomas admits this adventurous side of his nature is tempered by a need for financial security, which was a restricting influence at times. The main factors that helped him change career were flexibility and adaptability.

Thomas feels that people should pursue their ambitions wherever possible, even if that means taking risks. However, good planning and preparation together with good knowledge of your own strengths and weaknesses should reduce any risks involved. He has no plans for a further change of career at present but would not rule this out.

Having read through the case studies of successful career changers, certain patterns should be apparent.

Despite their diversity, many of the career changers reveal a history of successful job and career change.

Although often prompted by redundancy (voluntary or involuntary) the actual career change is usually based on a desire to change.

Many of the career changers faced serious obstacles to achieving their goals but all managed to overcome these by a combination of self-belief, determination, good planning and hard work.

The reasons for change usually included internal motives such as a desire for greater job satisfaction/fulfilment; to have a more worthwhile job; greater skills utilization; greater creative freedom and initiative and to meet new challenges.

The majority of changers had targeted a specific new occupation and moved toward this.

Once again, it is unlikely that any of the case studies quoted will exactly duplicate your own situation. However, there may be some similarities between your qualifications, experiences, motives, obstacles, or expectations, to make it worthwhile reflecting on appropriate cases and using them as models to assist you with your own planned change.

In many respects, unsuccessful career change attempts are similar to those that have more successful outcomes. However, there are also important differences. These should become apparent as you read the case studies presented in the next section of this chapter.

CASE STUDIES OF UNSUCCESSFUL CAREER CHANGERS

The case studies presented in this section focus on the experiences of individuals who have been unsuccessful in their attempts to change career. Table II overleaf gives brief details of the types of career changes participants in the study attempted to make and the reasons why they were unsuccessful.

The outlines of unsuccessful career change presented here are too varied to draw definite conclusions. However, discernible patterns are apparent. Many of the attempted career changes involve:

moves away from an existing career rather than a move towards a specified new career;

unrealistic goals;

TABLE II

UNSUCCESSFUL CAREER CHANGE ATTEMPTS: BRIEF OUTLINES				
Gender	Age at Attempt	Attempted to change from	Attempted to change to	Reasons for lack of success
Male	45	Civil Servant	Anything suitable	Pension; lack of opportunities; unsure which new career to pursue
Female	51	Computer programmer	Small hotel proprietor	Inadequate planning/financial problems
Male	38	Financial Advisor	Anything suitable	Lack of qualifications & opportunities
Male	38	Laboratory technician	Anything suitable	Family circumstances/lack of determination
Female	42	Industrial chemist	Management	Ageism, over-qualified lack of relevant experience
Male	48	Engineering	Public relations	Ageism/lack of opportunities
Male	39	Social worker	Teacher	Lack of relevant qualifications & experience; dislike of reduced status

a lack of planning and preparation;

inappropriate timing (e.g. when a pension would be jeopardized or when family circumstances made the proposed change inadvisable or unworkable);

a lack of relevant qualifications and/or work experience;

a lack of financial resources.

Brief outlines of unsuccessful career change attempts are a useful way to identify patterns common to many of the changers involved. However, to obtain a greater insight into why these attempts were unsuccessful, it is necessary to consider specific examples in greater detail. The following three case studies should prove useful in this respect.

CASE STUDY NO. 1

Jayne Harrison is a 42-year-old lecturer in a large further education college in the Midlands. She originally worked in the sales department of a large engineering company but left when her children were born because she needed more flexible employment. She spent five years working on a part-time basis before obtaining a permanent post.

Over the last five or six years Jayne has become very disillusioned with her job. The hours are now longer, the holidays shorter, and job security has been greatly reduced. Like many of her colleagues, Jayne is now keen to leave education and seek an alternative career. She dislikes the changes that have taken place and feels the situation will get worse. Motivation and job satisfaction are low and she feels frustrated by the worsening conditions of employment, lack of financial rewards and promotion prospects.

Jayne has been applying for posts outside teaching for the last 18 months, so far without success. Her main expectations for a new career are increased job security, improved financial rewards and status, better working conditions and greater job satisfaction. She has no clear goals and is keeping her options open. If anything "suitable" comes along that meets her requirements she will change her career. She is unwilling to consider another post in further education because she feels the same problems would apply.

The main obstacles she has encountered so far are her family circumstances; employers who are unwilling to accept mature applicants without the relevant qualifications, skills and work experience; and the lack of suitable job opportunities. Jayne still hopes to make a successful career change although she finds it difficult to have the time and energy to pursue her plans in her present circumstances.

CASE STUDY NO. 2

James Smith is 52 years of age and is currently employed as a production manager in a large food processing plant. He has had three employers and worked his way up from the shop floor to become a supervisor and then a production manager. He has acquired qualifications in supervisory and managerial areas and feels he has a wide variety of skills and experience at these levels.

James has been reassessing his career for a number of years and has been feeling increasingly dissatisfied with his current occupation. He has no definite alternative career in mind but would like to change to something where he can help people more.

He has recently completed an Open University degree which included options in Psychology and Sociology. His main motives for a career change are the desire for a more worthwhile job and to make better use of his recently acquired qualifications. His main expectations for a new career are greater feelings of job satisfaction and fulfilment.

He has no clear goals with regard to a possible new career but feels the main obstacles to a career change would be ageism (because he is now 52), the lengthy training periods involved for many occupations, and the problem of obtaining financial support for any training he decided to take. He also feels it would be difficult for him to start a new career on the bottom rungs of the ladder with (at least initially) a loss of financial reward and status.

His personal circumstances are favourable to a career change at this time. His three children have left home and are financially independent. His wife has a full-time job and he has completed his mortgage. In addition, he has been offered voluntary redundancy by his company which would provide a financial buffer whilst he pursued his career change.

Despite the problems he anticipates, he does intend to pursue a career change to one of the helping/caring professions.

CASE STUDY NO. 3

Mary Haines is 54 years of age and has been trying to change career for the last twelve years. Mary is an English graduate who followed a career in teaching and became head of English in a large comprehensive school.

Mary had always enjoyed her job as a teacher. The desire to change career occurred when her small school joined with a much larger school and the friendly atmosphere changed to one of

CAREER CHANGERS: THEIR MOTIVES, PROBLEMS AND EXPECTATIONS

conflict and mistrust. Soon after the merger, many of her colleagues from the smaller school left for other jobs and Mary felt increasingly isolated.

The increasing dissatisfaction with the job encouraged Mary to look for an alternative career. She had always been interested in publishing and decided to make this her new career. However, it proved far more difficult than expected. Mary has applied for numerous publishing jobs over the last ten years but so far without success.

Disillusioned with her teaching and despairing of a new career, Mary took early retirement when she was fifty. She is divorced, has no dependents and no mortgage. However, the drop in income was hard to adjust to and she decided to look for a part-time job.

Although she had not given up the pursuit of a job in publishing, in reality she knew her chances were diminishing all the time. Mary decided to take a temporary part-time post teaching English to mature adults in a local adult education centre. To her surprise she found this very enjoyable. She now works for two local colleges as well as the adult centre run by her local education authority.

Mary is beginning to realize that her decision to seek a new career may have been unnecessary. It was not teaching she was dissatisfied with, but the particular job and the increasing bureaucracy that accompanied it. Now she is working part-time with few administrative duties she feels relatively independent and is really enjoying her teaching again.

Mary was always motivated by job satisfaction rather than financial reward or status. She now realizes she wasted time pursuing an unrealistic career when she could have analysed her position more carefully and transferred to another school or to further and adult education a lot earlier.

Learning what to avoid is just as important as learning what to copy. The examples of "successful" and "unsuccessful" career changes presented in this chapter should provide useful models to guide you through your own proposed career change. In addition, they should serve to reinforce points made in earlier chapters about the importance of knowing yourself and knowing your market.

While there is no proven formula for making a successful career change, there are clearly some principles which (if followed) will greatly improve your chances of success. On the other hand, some approaches have less chance of success and should be avoided if possible.

One issue which has been continually emphasized throughout the book is the need for thorough planning and preparation. This is the focal point for chapter four.

CHAPTER FOUR

PLANNING FOR SUCCESS

Earlier chapters have laid the foundations for you to start planning your own career change. Chapter four draws together the key areas identified so far and focuses on the development and implementation of a strategic plan to help you succeed in your quest for an alternative career.

You should be aware by now that the key to a successful career change lies in knowledge – of yourself and the market. In addition, you have been given the opportunity to learn from the experiences of others – what to copy and what to avoid.

The final piece of the jigsaw is to demonstrate how you can use this knowledge to review the alternative career options selected and to decide which ones are attainable and how they should be pursued. The main aim of this chapter is to help you to set realistic career goals and achieve the career goals you set. It should be remembered that while there is no guarantee of success, the more carefully and thoroughly you research any proposed career change (in terms of its suitability and feasibility) the more you increase your chances of changing career and being satisfied with your new career.

To help you negotiate the difficult hurdles of strategic planning, the chapter is divided into five sections, as listed below.

Your personal marketing plan

Setting realistic goals

Pursuing realistic goals

Employment trends

MEM (Monitor. . . . .Evaluate. . . . .Modify)

Each section, whilst presenting new ideas and suggestions, also draws on and re-emphasizes important points made in earlier chapters. By adopting this approach it is hoped that readers will appreciate the sequential and overlapping nature of the stages presented and recognize the key issues involved in the accomplishment of a successful career change.

Your personal marketing plan

Chapter one encouraged self-knowledge and chapter two urged you to investigate potential new careers. The formulation of a personal marketing plan will help you to reap the benefits of any new information gained from these earlier chapters.

Some of you may already be familiar with the concept of marketing plans but associate these solely (or at least primarily) with business planning. The personal marketing plan adopts the same basic principles but targets them towards helping individuals to focus on their objectives in relation to career change and to specify how these can be achieved.

The format of the personal marketing plan, adapted for the purpose of career change, is in two parts. Part one outlines a strategy presented in the form of a flowchart. Part two provides the framework of a more detailed plan for you to complete. At each stage examples are provided to make the plan easier to complete. It is advisable to spend some time considering each aspect of the plan before committing your thoughts to paper.

Career change personal marketing plan

STAGE ONE: STRATEGY

CARRY OUT A PERSONAL SWOT ANALYSIS
(completed in Chapter two)

IDENTIFY CAREER CHANGE OBJECTIVES
(e.g. become self-employed; retrain as a systems analyst . . .)

FORMULATE STRATEGIES TO ACHIEVE OBJECTIVES
(e.g. join a "start a business" course; obtain a
bank loan or training grant)

SET A REALISTIC TIMESCALE FOR ACHIEVEMENT
(e.g. start trading within six months;

qualify within 2 years . . .)

DECIDE HOW/WHEN TO MONITOR PROGRESS
(e.g. keep a log book and review weekly . . .)

PUBLICIZE INTENTIONS
(e.g. announce to family and friends or
to business colleagues . . .)

IMPLEMENT THE "PERSONAL MARKETING PLAN"
(e.g. start the business or course . . .)

REGULARLY REVIEW/RECORD PROGRESS
(e.g. keep accurate accounts; note profits
or course work grades . . .)

REGULARLY CONGRATULATE/REWARD PROGRESS
(e.g. admit success to yourself and others;
book a short holiday . . .)

ACHIEVE CAREER OBJECTIVES
(e.g. achieve profit goals set;
successfully complete a course . . .)

The main purpose of completing stage one of the Personal Marketing Plan is to help you formalize your ideas and to develop a strategy for achieving the objectives you decide to set. To simplify the process and avoid confusion, it is advisable to complete a separate plan for each objective you specify.

A crucial aspect of strategic planning, often neglected, is the monitoring and feedback aspect. It is unlikely that any plan will proceed smoothly from the outset. Often it is difficult to set realistic objectives until we have actually embarked on a plan. Alternatively, unexpected events may force us to deviate from our plan (for example in terms of timescale) or to abandon a plan altogether.

Setbacks will occur and it is important to account for these during the early stages of planning and preparation. This will lessen the impact when difficulties arise and make it easier to switch to alternative routes or even alternative objectives.

INTERNAL CAREER CHANGE

Changing career within your existing organization requires as much planning as external career change. Chapter two outlined the main advantages and disadvantages of internal career change. If you decide to attempt this type of career change the key points identified below should prove beneficial.

Carry out provisional research to find out:

if internal career change is feasible within your organization;

what procedures you must follow to accomplish an internal career change.

If your organization encourages or accommodates internal career change and has an established set of procedures, then it will be much easier for you to pursue this path. However, if this is not the case, then you will need to sell the idea of internal career change to your employers as well as sell yourself as a suitable candidate for such change.

Contact the appropriate people to make them aware of your desire to explore different career directions. Useful ways to initiate discussion include:

contact your personnel department;

raise the issue at your next annual appraisal;

speak to your line manager;

perhaps operate informally by exploring the possibility of change with the managers of the departments you are targeting for change;

through departmental representatives (if available);

through trades union representatives (if available).

If you need to sell the idea of internal career change, it is essential to focus on the potential benefits for the organization. These would include:

the reduced opportunities for vertical progression has increased the need for sideways moves as a way of ensuring "mobility" within the workforce;

in a period of rapid change it is essential for workers to be multi-skilled and to operate a flexible system of staff development;

it is useful to rotate/second staff at regular intervals and let other areas gain from their existing experience and skills;

to prevent the loss of valuable workers who seek career progress outside your organization;

to boost staff morale and increase job satisfaction and motivation.

To sell yourself as a suitable candidate for an internal career change you could:

take advantage of any relevant opportunities for training and development offered by your employers;

initiate and fund your own training and development to emphasize your commitment to career change;

research internal career change practices within other organizations and bring these to the attention of your management;

use relevant journal or newspaper articles to support your case for internal career change.

The more carefully you research the possibilities for internal career change and support these with evidence showing the benefits to your employer, the more likely you are to succeed.

Stage two of the plan provides a framework within which to analyse more precisely what you are trying to achieve and to specify how you intend to achieve your stated objectives. Once again examples are provided to illustrate the type of information required for the different elements of the framework. The framework may be difficult to complete initially but should help you to structure your plans in a constructive and productive way.

CAREER CHANGE PERSONAL MARKETING PLAN
STAGE TWO: FRAMEWORK

OBJECTIVES
(restate e.g. to become self-employed . . .)

STRATEGY
(how you aim to achieve your stated objectives
e.g. work from home on a part-time basis until
you have sufficient clients and money to
operate full-time from rented premises . . .)

MARKETING MIX

PLACE
(e.g. work from home; rent or buy premises in a technology park; rent a shop in a busy shopping centre. . .)

PROMOTION
(e.g. advertise in a local newspaper; distribute leaflets; advertise in local directories)

PRICE
(e.g. if a hairdresser, what prices would you charge for the services and products provided to customers . . .)

PRODUCT
(e.g. if a hairdresser what services would you provide for customers and what type of hair products would you sell . . .)

IMPLEMENTATION
(when you put your plans into action e.g. actually start working from home or buy or rent premises and start trading . . . .)

The examples given as part of stage two of your Personal Marketing Plan relate to setting up a business. This example was used to clearly illustrate the requirements of the plan. You may find it more difficult to adapt this framework to paid employment. However, the basic principles are the same as the two examples presented below illustrate.

Example one:

Objective:	to retrain as a systems analyst
Strategy:	to obtain a one year unpaid leave of absence from present job to join a full-time systems analyst course. Fees and a grant are available for this retraining programme
Place:	University of Liverpool
Promotion:	write to the University stating interest in the course and convince them of your suitability during a personal visit
Price:	the grant that is available whilst attending the course
Product:	the systems analyst course

Example Two:

Objective:	to obtain a position as a college lecturer or training instructor in a private agency
Strategy:	obtain part-time work to build up skills and contacts; obtain the necessary OSC awards to teach and assess on NVQ and GNVQ courses
Place:	a further education college or private training agency within a 20 mile radius of home
Promotion:	send a CV and accompanying letter to all education and training establishments in the target area; network with existing lecturers and tutors
Price:	require a payment rate of between twelve and fourteen pounds an hour
Product:	lecturer or trainer in bookkeeping and accounts

The personal marketing plan formats used in this section should provide a useful basis on which to plan your proposed career change. If several new careers are under consideration then each option will require separate plans.

The main purpose of these plans is to encourage you to commit your ideas to paper and be precise about *what* you wish to achieve, *how* you intend to achieve it, and *when* you intend to achieve it. All plans should be flexible and should be reviewed and revised regularly, according to the progress you have made.

The more time you spend developing your career change proposals the more accurately you will be able to judge the feasibility of your objectives. The more realistic your objectives the greater your chance of success.

SETTING REALISTIC GOALS

A crucial first step when planning a change of career is to conduct a candid evaluation of your strengths and weaknesses in relation to favoured occupations. The exercises contained in chapter one provided a provisional opportunity for this. However, it is now necessary to review any conclusions reached at that stage in the light of further insight gained through subsequent chapters.

A useful way to carry out this review is to answer the ten questions posed below as honestly as possible given your current knowledge and understanding of both yourself and the market you are attempting to enter.

Question One: given a completely free choice which occupation would you choose?
(e.g. catwalk model, actor, jockey . . .)

Question Two: what would prevent you from actually succeeding at the occupation named as your ideal choice?
(e.g. not tall enough, too timid, fear of horses . . .)

Question Three: why was your ideal career so attractive?
(e.g. material rewards, fame, competitive nature . . .)

Question Four: what other occupations could satisfy your needs – to a lesser extent?
(e.g. public relations, advertising, marketing, barrister, solicitor . . .)

Question Five: what would prevent you from entering these (alternative) occupations?
(e.g. too much competition, long training periods, lack of relevant qualifications . . .)

Question Six: how could you overcome the barriers to entry that you have identified?
(e.g. effective networking, study part-time, part-time or voluntary work to gain relevant experience)

Question Seven: what might prevent you from overcoming the barriers identified?
(e.g. lack of useful contacts, lack of confidence in your ability, insufficient time to devote to study, lack of opportunity for relevant work experience . . .)

Question Eight: which occupations could meet many of your needs and be relatively easy to enter?
(e.g. sales, receptionist, teacher, demonstrator, beauty

therapist . . .)

Question Nine: are these occupations ones you have seriously considered joining?
(yes or no)

Question Ten: if you have not seriously considered these occupations before, why not?
(e.g. too ordinary, not exciting enough, salary too low, lack of prospects, thought you could be better . . .)

IDEAL V REALISTIC CAREERS

To understand what something *is* it is useful to start by identifying what it *is not*. Applied to career change this principle should help you to establish and strive towards *realistic goals*.

The purpose of answering the ten questions posed earlier was to help you to draw up a scale with your ideal career at one end and more mundane but more realistic alternatives at the opposite end. An example of this is given below:

IDEAL CAREER   **REALISTIC CAREER**
Actor   Demonstrator

Naming an "ideal career" should have helped you to discover why this career was so appealing but also why it was virtually impossible to achieve. By gradually refocusing on the key features of your ideal career it should be possible to identify alternative careers that have similar features but without the highly prized rewards such as fame, wealth and status. These "scaled down" versions of an ideal career should be far more attainable and thus represent the realistic goals which are the focus of this chapter.

Emphasizing the importance of realistic goals is not meant to convey a negative message concerning aspirations. The aim is not to curb ambition or to deter effort, but to encourage individuals to honestly assess their chances of achieving any career goals they set.

PURSUING REALISTIC GOALS

For some people, goal-setting needs to be staged so that targets are set in the short, medium and long term. This makes goals easier to achieve than if one, fairly long-term goal is set. It is also advisable to consider alternative goals in case your preferred goals prove unattainable. Having "back-up" goals should lessen the fear of failure and the disappointment when setbacks occur.

It is now possible to define a realistic goal as an aim or target which is attainable, achievable or tenable. The ability to set realistic goals is usually associated with self-knowledge and knowledge of the market (both of which have been covered in earlier chapters). Achieving realistic goals does not follow automatically but is the result of careful planning and preparation.

An increasingly important part of planning and preparation is the capability to investigate and consider future trends. Rapid changes are taking place within organizations and industries, often in response to economic, political and technological change. An occupation which is viable today may have a relatively short lifespan. This needs to be taken into account when considering a change of career.

Examples of industries currently undergoing radical change include banking, education, electricity, gas, local government, postal services, retail, telecommunications and transport. Many occupations have adopted or are considering the use of contract employees rather than offering permanent, full-time jobs – a trend which is likely to continue.

Thorough research into current and anticipated trends is essential before embarking on a new career. This is particularly relevant in the case of occupations which involve a fairly lengthy training period. You need to know what job opportunities are likely to be available when the training is complete.

In some occupations, it may be necessary or preferable to have more than one employer. In other instances, occupations themselves may operate in parallel. The main advantage to these trends is the flexibility provided for workers who, increasingly, need to accept responsibility for their own career development. The main disadvantage is the lack of security and the effect this has on pensions, insurance and salaries.

One consequence of these trends is that in addition to considering alternative occupations, career changers also need to research the type of industries and organizations in which they hope to gain employment.

To assist with this task, the next two sections focus on occupations that are worth pursuing and those that should be approached with caution.

EMPLOYMENT TRENDS, OPPORTUNITIES AND OBSTACLES

Given the current, changeable nature of the economy and organizational structures, it is impossible to provide a definitive list of occupations that should be avoided.

The main theme of the book so far has been one of "guided discovery" – of yourself and the occupations you may wish to enter. The adoption of this theme is justified when the complex issue of career choice is considered.

For many readers, the type of self-help encouraged by the book will be sufficient. Others may find the book useful in taking the first (often tentative) steps towards investigating alternative careers and setting realistic goals. If further, more individual, advice and support is required, you should contact one of the private or public recruitment agencies or careers advisory services, established for this purpose.

EMPLOYMENT TRENDS IN THE UNITED KINGDOM

Before identifying specific careers to approach with caution, it is useful to consider current patterns or trends in employment. Surveys of employment trends are conducted regularly. The summary of findings listed below highlights industries and occupations currently in decline. As a consequence, job opportunities are likely to be limited.

Although a continued recovery in the labour market is forecast by the Labour Force Survey, a change in the nature of jobs available is anticipated. Taking a broad industrial perspective, employment in primary and utility industries (such as agriculture, mining, gas and water) is expected to decline by 12% between 1993 and 2001, with an 8% decline in manufacturing.

The trend away from full-time employment with an employer (currently around 62% of total employment) is also projected to continue, with a further decrease of 0.3 million reducing the figure to

57% by 2001. Conversely, the number of part-time jobs (currently around 24% of employment) is likely to increase by an extra 1.3 million by 2001 taking the figure to 28%.

Low-skilled manual occupations are expected to fall by more than half a million between 1993 and 2001. The increasing flexibility within employment means that workers with narrow skills will find it difficult to obtain jobs. Appropriate qualifications (such as NVQs, GNVQs, technical and academic) are now required for most jobs.

BARRIERS TO EMPLOYMENT

The research findings and related case studies quoted earlier show that career obstacles can be overcome. Being aware of potential obstacles is a crucial first step towards this. The list presented below identifies potential barriers to career change which should be investigated in relation to specific occupations. These are:

age

geographical region

lack of relevant qualifications

lack of relevant work experience

Age is often cited as a barrier to employment. In some instances a worker may be considered too young for a particular post. However, in most cases it is older workers who face discrimination. Unfortunately, as mentioned earlier, age discrimination is not illegal within the United Kingdom at the present time. Many employers place upper age ceilings on posts, whilst others reject older applicants on the grounds of their lack of relevant qualifications and/or work experience. Strategies to combat age discrimination include omitting age from an application form and CV; stating age but justifying the application on the grounds of suitability for the job; or only applying for jobs which encourage (or at least do not deter) older applicants. Alternatively, mature individuals may be able to overcome age restrictions by indicating their willingness to accept a short-term contract for a trial period.

Geographical region can be a barrier to employment in a depressed area or one that is too small or remote to attract many employers. If you are geographically mobile the solution may be to seek employment in more prosperous areas (either by moving house or living away from home during work periods). If you are geographically immobile, home-based employment may be the solution.

Lack of relevant qualifications is increasingly a barrier to employment due partly to the rapid technological changes that are taking place, and partly to the emphasis now put on formal qualifications by employers. To overcome this type of barrier it is important to engage in continuing professional development and to be prepared to retrain if this is required by an alternative occupation.

Lack of relevant work experience often acts as a barrier to employment, especially if a new career is the target. There are a number of ways to overcome this problem: engage in relevant voluntary activities to gain the necessary experience; try to gain some relevant experience within an existing career and hope that this is recognized by employers; be prepared to accept an initial reduction in pay and status to gain the necessary experience and skills.

Approaching a change of occupation with caution is an essential part of the planning and preparation process. It is not an indication of negative thought, pessimism or defeatism but an indication that you have the ability to view your position objectively, evaluate your chances of success and set realistic goals.

CAREERS WITH POTENTIAL

Once again, published statistics on employment trends in the UK are a useful general guide to the industries and occupations where vacancies are likely to occur. The following points indicate the current patterns of UK employment at the present time.

According to the Labour Force Survey, long-term employment growth can be expected. Projections suggest a growth of 0.6% a year up to 1997 followed by a growth of 0.9% a year to 2001, which represents a total of 1.6 million extra jobs by 2001.

In 1993 almost 45% of all jobs were in the service sectors (private and public) and over 25% in distributive industries. This trend is likely to continue to 2001.

Between 1993 and 2001 employment in the construction industry is projected to increase by 7%, distribution and transport by 6%, business and miscellaneous services by 23% and public services by 8%.

Higher level occupations are showing the fastest growth. Between 1993 and 2001 almost 1.7 million extra managerial, professional and technician level jobs are expected to appear. In 1993, these higher level occupations accounted for 35% of total employment and this figure is expected to rise to over 39% by 2001. Even where jobs are declining in numbers, there will be a need for new workers because of job changes and retirement. This may particularly affect vital intermediate level occupations (such as in the skilled engineering trades) (Skills and Enterprise Network, 1995).

"Skill shortages" are an important indicator of occupations in which vacancies are likely to exist. Most of the "hard to fill" vacancies are in the higher skills content occupations, such as craft and related occupations; personal and protective services; catering occupations; textiles, garments and related trades; health associate professionals; sales representatives; engineers and technicians (Labour Market Quarterly Report, November 1993).

When industries are considered, the number of "hard to fill" vacancies reported by employers is a good indicator of current employment prospects. However, the position can change fairly quickly. In 1994, the main reported shortages were in hotel and catering (27%); banking (22%); textiles, clothing and footwear (21%); medical and other health services (16%); distribution and consumer services (14%); metal goods (14%); office machinery electrical (12%); research and development and other services (12%); recreational and personal services (11%); general engineering (11%); motor vehicles/transport equipment (11%) and mechanical engineering (10%). (Skills and Enterprise Briefing, November 1994).

The trend away from full-time and towards part-time employment favours women. Part-time jobs (which are expected to rise from 24% of employment to 28% by 2001) are predominantly taken by women, and the number of female workers is expected to increase by over 1.2 million during this period. By 2001 women will constitute 52% of all employees (Skills and Enterprise Network, 1995).

Self-employment showed strong growth in the 1980s. This trend was (temporarily) interrupted by the recession, but is expected to resume. It is estimated that over 0.5 million more people will be self-employed by 2000 (Skills and Enterprise Network, 1995).

Small firms account for a growing proportion of employment. In the decade from 1979 to 1989 their numbers grew from 1.9 million to 3.1 million and they provided the vast majority of new jobs in the 1980s. Once again, this growth was (temporarily) halted by the recession but has now resumed. One reason for this growth is the increasing tendency for larger firms to contract out peripheral aspects, often to smaller businesses and the self-employed (Skills and Enterprise Network, 1995).

COMBATTING AGEISM IN EMPLOYMENT

Drawing attention to ageism in employment is necessary since many of those planning (or hoping) to change career would be classified (by employers) as "older workers". As mentioned before, age discrimination is not illegal in the United Kingdom. It is practised by many employers: older workers generally have a negative image in relation to health, flexibility and trainability and as a group they are an obvious, convenient target for redundancy and early retirement.

A study of job advertisements will reveal that many employers either state an upper age limit for applicants, or indirectly deter older applicants by their stated requirements and job descriptions. The government and bodies such as the CBI (Confederation of British Industries) and IPD (Institute of Personnel and Development) have advocated a change in recruitment policy towards older workers, so far with limited success.

Some employers have adopted a positive attitude towards older applicants, to the extent of deliberately encouraging them. It is neither possible nor appropriate for this book to provide detailed information on which organizations are willing to accept older recruits for specific careers. However, by providing examples of employers who encourage older applicants it should help readers to identify which companies to approach when seeking employment (Naylor, 1990; Employment Department, 1994). The list of employers given here is not exhaustive. Job Centres, job advertisements and careers advisors are useful additional sources of information.

Examples of public sector employers who recruit older workers include local authorities, the police service, education, social work, the prison service, some civil service and British Rail posts and other public sector employers.

Examples of private sector employers who encourage older applicants include Unigate plc, B & Q, Texaco Limited, National Westminster Bank, Sainsbury's, Tesco, Gateway, The Dixons Group, Trust House Forte, De Vere and Thistle Hotels. The clearing banks and high street building societies have targeted women returners for special consideration with the Midland Bank and Nationwide Building Society receiving wide publicity for their schemes in this area.

Some organizations have adopted policies to enable older workers to be accepted into technical apprenticeship schemes or other similar training programmes. These include British Telecom, Peugeot Talbot, British Rail and the Ford Motor Company. In addition, the NHS, the Wellcome Trust, Scotrail and Boots have introduced schemes to improve the recruitment, development and retention of young and middle-aged staff. Other companies, such as IBM, operate a "Skill Base" programme under which older workers who accept early retirement are offered a quota of work from the company.

As well as the organizations referred to, a number of agencies concerned with the placement of older workers have appeared in Britain over the last few years. These often specialize in the recruitment of higher grade staff, such as managers and professionals.

TRANSFERABLE SKILLS

In many instances, although workers may lack the specific skills required for particular jobs, they do possess a wealth of work-related skills which could easily be transferred to other jobs and occupations. Increased recognition of this and the availability of mechanisms to accommodate such transfers have helped to create greater occupational mobility. Examples of such mechanisms include APL and APE (accreditation of prior learning and experience); OSC (Occupational Standards Council) formerly TDLB (Training and Development Lead Body); MCI (Management Charter Initiative).

At the heart of these mechanisms is the production and presentation of a portfolio containing evidence of specific skills matched against relevant statements of competence. The growing acceptance of such portfolios has led to the emergence of more informal "management" and "career development" portfolios which may be used to convince employers of an applicant's ability to perform a job for which they are not formally qualified or trained.

Acquiring relevant qualifications

It is now possible to acquire many academic and vocational qualifications on a part-time, open, distance or flexible learning basis. The Open University and Open College Federation together with numerous further and higher educational establishments now offer many courses that are geared towards their students' busy lifestyles. These courses are of varying duration (from a few days to a few years), levels (from GCSEs to MBAs) and cover a wide range of subjects (from computers to health care; floristry to nursery nursing).

The wide range and flexible nature of the courses offered make it relatively easy to retrain completely or to engage in professional updating. Some courses target specific groups (such as women returners, unemployed graduates, unemployed executives, or people wishing to start their own businesses). In some cases, grants or sponsorship are available; if unemployed, the courses are usually free; or if payment is required, student loans or instalment arrangements are usually available.

Even if lengthy training is required to change occupation, embarking on a relevant course of study or partial completion may be sufficient to persuade an organization to employ you, provided you were prepared to complete the necessary programme.

Self-employment

The reported increase in self-employment over recent years is partly in response to increases in redundancies and early retirements, and partly a result of improved assistance to small businesses.

If you decide to change career in this direction, the book should provide a good indication of your suitability for self-employment (for example in terms of motivation, coping with stress, ability to work alone, necessary skills etc.), and the existence of a market for the product or service you wish to offer.

If, as a result of self-assessment and market research, you decide to pursue self-employment, it is essential to obtain expert advice at an early stage of your planning and preparation. This would include advice from an accountant, solicitor and bank manager. In addition, it is advisable to contact your local TEC to find out about the type and nature of help available to new and small businesses with regard to finance, support and training. Other, more specialized, advice may be necessary depending on the nature of your proposed business.

As you have seen, Employment Surveys show some encouraging trends which, if they materialize, should provide increased opportunities for career change. Targeting occupations with the potential for growth should greatly increase your chance of making a successful career change. This is especially true if you keep monitoring and reviewing your progress as outlined in the final section of this chapter.

MEM (MONITOR . . . EVALUATE . . . MODIFY)

A crucial aspect of planning and preparation is to periodically try to stand back from your task and take an objective look at the results achieved to date. Because it is difficult to view our own work objectively, it is often useful to enlist the help of a third party – preferably someone who knows you and your plans. To be effective, any feedback you receive (either from yourself or from relevant others) should be acted upon.

To emphasize the importance of this "stocktaking" exercise and to encourage you to employ this strategy on a regular basis, this final section is divided into three main parts which reflect the MEM of the title – Monitor, Evaluate, Modify.

MONITOR

"Monitoring" in this context means to continually (or at least periodically) check the progress made in your attempt to change career. This should be relatively simple if you are working to a plan as suggested. However, in the absence of a plan, monitoring, although far more difficult, becomes even more important.

Without regular monitoring you are likely to waste time and energy pursuing goals that are not achievable. With regular monitoring you should be able to detect or even anticipate difficulties before they become too serious. The need for monitoring is generally accepted in the workplace as the following examples illustrate:

on a production line progress is continually monitored either by the workers themselves, a line supervisor or by some computerized or mechanical means;

in a sales department, follow-up telephone calls or letters are often used to gain sales;

in an accounts department, payments are monitored to compile a list of non-payers so that reminders can be sent;

in a hospital, patient progress is continually monitored and recorded on charts and patient records;

in a garage, an intermittent fault on a car will be monitored to help the mechanic pinpoint where the problem lies.

Unfortunately, people are often less systematic when it comes to monitoring their personal or career goals. The excuses given for this are usually quite genuine – insufficient time, too many conflicting commitments, unforeseen events and crises, unwelcome interruptions, unco-operative contacts. . . . However, the consequences of not monitoring on a regular basis can be serious (even disastrous).

Some people find it much easier to be systematic and well-organized than others. To them, monitoring would be almost an automatic process. For others, who may lead a generally disorganized existence, monitoring would be quite alien and require far more planning and effort.

An honest appraisal of personal and family circumstances should have been conducted in chapter one and the findings incorporated into your career change plan. Any obvious deficiencies should have been recognized and mechanisms put into place to counteract these. Examples of these mechanisms would include:

drawing up a written timetable by which certain stages of your plan should be achieved;

delegating certain tasks to others (such as husband/wife, father, mother, friend, business colleague);

outlining the specific tasks to be achieved each day or week;

disciplining yourself to meet short-term (or very short-term) goals;

arranging for other people to remind you to carry out the tasks set.

Monitoring, although a useful exercise, is inadequate on its own. To be truly effective, the results of your monitoring need to be evaluated and acted upon.

EVALUATE

Monitoring your progress, even if only on an informal basis, will provide information about developments in your plan to change career. When you have this information it is important to carry out some form of analysis, review or appraisal to find out if you are on target to achieve your goals. The main aims of this evaluation are:

to identify obstacles to your career change plans;

to discover why these obstacles exist;

to find ways to overcome any obstacles identified;

to consider radically changing or abandoning your current plans.

The following examples should help to illustrate these points.

Example One: you may be experiencing difficulty financing a retraining course. The reason for this difficulty is that you have already received your full quota of financial assistance from your local education authority. Ways to overcome this difficulty include obtaining a student loan, paying for the course yourself, or obtaining sponsorship from an employer.

Example Two: you have been refused a bank loan to use as start-up capital in a small business venture. The reason for this rejection is your lack of collateral. Ways to overcome this difficulty include seeking a business partner(s), postponing the venture until you can earn money to finance yourself, operate initially on a part-time basis, or seek finance elsewhere.

Example Three: you have applied for 50 vacancies in your chosen alternative occupation but have not yet received an interview. The reason for your lack of success is insufficient relevant work experience. Ways to overcome this difficulty include gaining some relevant experience on a part-time or voluntary basis, or convincing prospective employers that your current skills and experiences are sufficient.

Example Four: you have become self-employed but are experiencing difficulty attracting clients. The main reasons for this include too many competitors, poor publicity and the lack of a clear marketing plan. Ways to overcome this difficulty include seeking advice from your local

TEC or business enterprise agency, enrolling on a business course, networking with others in the same line of business, and conducting a well-organized marketing campaign.

Example Five: you have retrained in your new career but find jobs are only available in another part of the country. The main reasons for this include closures or redundancies by local firms. Ways to overcome this difficulty include relocation, or live away from home during the working week and return home at weekends.

The difficulties identified in these five examples are fairly extreme and could mainly have been avoided by thorough planning and preparation. However, at least by monitoring and evaluating your progress, the difficulties have been highlighted and possible solutions identified. In some cases, it will not be possible to overcome the obstacles and current plans may have to be radically modified or even abandoned.

MODIFY

The advantage of continually monitoring and evaluating your career change plans is that difficulties may be identified and attended to before they become too serious. However, recognizing a difficulty and being prepared (or able) to overcome it are two different issues. In many cases, if identified early enough, difficulties can be overcome with only relatively minor alterations to your plans. Examples of such alterations may include:

seeking alternative training courses;

seeking alternative sources of finance;

engaging in part-time or voluntary work to gain relevant work experience;

obtaining professional advice on how to market your product or service;

registering with an executive job club to help you find employment.

However, in some instances it may be necessary to radically modify your plans or abandon them completely. This might be necessary under the following circumstances:

if you could not find employment in your chosen field;

if you were unable to attract sufficient clients to make a business viable;

if you could not pass the necessary examinations (or obtain the required grades);

if you were geographically immobile and job opportunities did not exist within your area;

It is always disappointing if radical changes have to be made or plans need to be abandoned completely. However, it is important to keep things in perspective and not view yourself as a "failure" because particular goals have not been met. It may be that your alternative career was not a good match to your skills and personal characteristics; perhaps your family circumstances prevented the change; or the timing of the change may have been wrong. Whatever the reason, it is important to strive for a positive outcome: if it is necessary to alter or abandon your plans then take action immediately to prevent further delays and disappointments.

Taken together, the three components of MEM (Monitor, Evaluate, Modify) are powerful tools to help you achieve your ultimate goal, even if this is not your original goal. The MEM process accommodates, even encourages, change whilst helping you to reach a successful conclusion.

CONCLUSION

Changing career is an option being considered by an increasing number of workers. For some it is a purely voluntary move, whilst for others it is a result of redundancy, early retirement and limited job opportunities in an existing occupation.

The message conveyed through this book is one of self-help. The more you know and understand about yourself and your proposed new occupation, the more likely you are to succeed. However, knowledge and understanding alone are not sufficient: you must also be prepared to put what you know into practice. It is this combination, the balance between thought and action that provides the key to a successful career change.

Changing career has been likened to finding your way through a maze. The following flowchart outlines a route or pathway which should help you travel through this maze without too much hardship and to emerge relatively unscathed at the other end.

ROUTE TO A SUCCESSFUL CAREER CHANGE

DECIDE TO CHANGE CAREER

CARRY OUT AN AUDIT OF YOUR ABILITIES, SKILLS
QUALIFICATIONS AND WORK EXPERIENCES

REFLECT ON YOUR CAREER MOTIVATIONS/
EXPECTATIONS

REFLECT ON WHAT YOU LIKE(D) MOST/LEAST ABOUT
YOUR
CURRENT (OR LAST) JOB/OCCUPATION

DECIDE ON TWO OR THREE NEW CAREERS THAT ARE
A GOOD MATCH TO YOUR
CAPABILITIES AND REQUIREMENTS

THOROUGHLY RESEARCH JOB
REQUIREMENTS AND OPPORTUNITIES
FOR THE ALTERNATIVE CAREERS IDENTIFIED

IDENTIFY FACTORS LIKELY TO HELP YOU
CHANGE CAREER

IDENTIFY THE MAIN OBSTACLES TO CHANGING CAREER

PLAN YOUR CAREER CHANGE CAREFULLY

SET REALISTIC GOALS/TIMESCALES
FOR THEIR ACHIEVEMENT

CONTINUALLY MONITOR YOUR PROGRESS AND MAKE
ADJUSTMENTS TO YOUR PLANS IF NECESSARY

CELEBRATE YOUR SUCCESSFUL CAREER CHANGE

CONTINUALLY MONITOR EMPLOYMENT TRENDS,
UPDATE
YOUR SKILLS/QUALIFICATIONS REGULARLY, AND BE
PREPARED TO MAKE FURTHER CAREER CHANGES
IF NECESSARY OR DESIRABLE

Success in any venture cannot be guaranteed. A successful career change will depend on the interaction of numerous variables of which some (such as the economic climate, job opportunities within a particular occupation, and rapid technological change) are outside your control. However, the more carefully you research and plan your change, the greater your chance of success.

BIBLIOGRAPHY

Cartwright, S. and Cooper, C.L. (1994), *No Hassle: Taking the Stress Out of Work*, London: Century Business.

Driver, J. (1979), *The Penguin Dictionary of Psychology*, Penguin Books Limited, England.

Employment Department (1994), *Labour Market Quarterly Report*, November, Skills and Enterprise Network Publications, Sheffield.

Hilgard, J., Atkinson, R.C. and Atikinson, R.L. (1975), *Introduction to Psychology*, Harcourt Brace, Jovanovich, USA.

Holland, J.L. *et al.*, (1973), "Applying an Occupational Classification to a Representative Sample of Work Histories", *Journal of Applied Psychology*, 58, 1.

Holmes, T. and Cartwright, S. (1993), "Career Change: Myth or Reality?" *Employee Relations*. Vol. 15, No. 6, 37–53.

Holmes, T. and Cartwright, S. (1994), "Mid-Career Change: the Ingredients for Success", *Employee Relations*, Vol. 16, No. 7.

Hopson, B. and Scally, M. (1984), *Build Your Own Rainbow*, Leeds: Lifeskill Associates.

Labour Force Survey (1989), *Training in Britain*, HMSO.

Labour Market Quarterly Report (1993), (November), Skills and Enterprise Network Publication, Sheffield.

Levensen, H. (1974), "Activism and Powerful Others: Distinctions within the Concept of Internal-External Control", *Journal of Personality*, 38, 377–383.

McCrae, R.R. and Costa, P.T. (1987), "Validation of the Five Factor Model of Personality across Instruments and Observers", *Journal of Personality and Social Psychology*, 52, 81–90.

Murgatroyd, S. (1988) *Counselling and Helping*, BPS Books/Methuen, London.

Nelson-Bolles, R. (1989), *What Color is Your Parachute?* New York: Ten Speed Press.

Naylor, P. (1990), *Age No Barrier*, METRA, England.

Roe, A. (1956), *The Psychology of Occupations*, John Wiley and Sons Inc., New York.

Rotter, J.B. (1966), "Generalised Expectancies for Internal versus External Control of Reinforcement", *Psychological Monographs General and Applied*, Whole Number 009.

Skills and Enterprise Briefing (1994), Issue 16/94 (November), Skills and Enterprise Network Publication, Sheffield.

Skills and Enterprise Briefing (1995), Skills and Enterprise Network Publication, Sheffield.

Social Trends (1990), Central Statistics Office, HMSO, London.

Social Trends (1991). Central Statistics Office, HMSO, London.

Spector, P.E. (1988), "Development of the Work Locus of Control Scale", *Journal of Occupational Psychology*, 61, 335–340.

Studner, P.K. (1989) *Super Job Search*, London: Mercury Books.

APPENDIX ONE

PSYCHOLOGICAL CHARACTERISTICS RATINGS SCALE SCORING SCHEDULE

LOW   MEDIUM   HIGH
1   2   3   4   5

SECTION A: INTROVERSION v EXTRAVERSION

Low scores indicate a tendency towards INTROVERSION and high scores a tendency towards EXTRAVERSION

SECTION B: HIGH ANXIETY v LOW ANXIETY

Low scores indicate a tendency towards HIGH ANXIETY and high scores a tendency towards LOW ANXIETY

SECTION C: OPENNESS TO EXPERIENCE

Low scores indicate a tendency to DISLIKE NEW EXPERIENCES and high scores a tendency to LIKE NEW EXPERIENCES

SECTION D: AGREEABLENESS v ANTAGONISM

Low scores indicate a tendency towards AGREEABLENESS and high scores a tendency towards ANTAGONISM

SECTION E: HIGH CONTROL v LOW CONTROL

Low scores indicate a tendency towards HIGH SELF-CONTROL and high scores a tendency towards LOW SELF-CONTROL

APPENDIX TWO
MOTIVATION PRIORITY SCALE SCORING SCHEDULE

This is not a "schedule" in the true sense since readers were asked to list and prioritize their own motives.

To obtain an indication of whether you are motivated "internally" or "externally" look back at the explanations and examples of these terms. Identify which of your motives may be considered internal and external and note the priority given to this item.

Example:

Internal Motives	External Motives	Scale Priority
The desire for greater job satisfaction		1
	More job perks	5
A greater sense of achievement		2
	Better promotion prospects	6
Greater independence		3
A more worthwhile job		4
	Improved working conditions	7
A greater challenge		8
	Improved status	9
	Improved basic salary	10

In the above example, since most priority is given to "internal" motives then we can assume that the person completing this scale would be happiest in a job that met their internal needs, although they also clearly expressed the need for a variety of external factors as well.

Using this as an example, analyse your own motives for work.

APPENDIX THREE

SPECTOR LOCUS OF CONTROL SCORING SCHEDULE

When completing the scale you were asked to respond on a scale 1–6 as follows:

1 = disagree very much   2 = disagree moderately
3 = disagree slightly   4 = agree slightly
5 = agree moderately   6 = agree very much

Half of your scores are equal to the value of the response you made. For example, if you responded 1 then your score for this item would be 1; or if you responded 5 then your score for this item would be 5. However, the other half of scores are worth the opposite of your response. For example if you responded 1 then your score for that item would 6; if you responded 3 the score would be 4 (this is known as REVERSE SCORING).

The item numbers that are worth the REVERSE of the response are 1, 2, 3, 4, 7, 11, 14 and 15. In all other instances, the scores are worth the same value as the response.

Example:

Item 1 you have responded "5" therefore your score would be 2
Item 6 you have responded "2" therefore your score would be 2

Go through your list of scores and mark their value (preferably in a different colour). When this is complete, add up your scores (by adding the value of responses for each item) and note this.

SPECTOR identifies a norm for this scale of 38.1. Scores below this figure (e.g. 20.5 or 35.4) would indicate a high INTERNAL LOCUS OF CONTROL. Scores above this figure (e.g. 46.9 or 66.2) would indicate a high EXTERNAL LOCUS OF CONTROL. The further your score is above or below the norm score the more extreme your locus of control in the direction indicated.

EXPECTATIONS PRIORITY SCALE SCORING SCHEDULE

This is not a "schedule" in the true sense since readers were allowed to insert additional expectations to the list provided before ranking these in order of priority.

Upon completion of the "ranking" exercise, readers should have access to two types of information about their career expectations: (1) the priority given to specific career expectations and (2) whether or not they gave priority to expectations linked to internal or external values.

Expectations based on internal values would relate to those concerned with the nature of the job or career itself, whereas expectations based on external values would relate to factors extraneous to the job tasks.

Example:

Internal Expectations	External Expectations	Scale Priority
Greater fulfilment/job satisfaction		1
	More job perks	5
A greater sense of achievement		2
	Better promotion prospects	6
Greater autonomy		3
A more worthwhile job		4
	Improved working conditions	7
Greater role identity		8
	Improved status	9
	Greater financial rewards	10

APPENDIX FIVE

THE FACILITATORY/INHIBITORY RATINGS SCALE SCORING SCHEDULE

When completing the scale you were asked to respond on a scale 1–6 as follows:

1 = strongly agree   2 = agree

3 = uncertain   4 = disagree

5 = strongly agree

The scale is designed to assess the extent to which you have a POSITIVE or NEGATIVE attitude towards career change.

When scoring item numbers 1, 2, 4, 5, 8 and 12 the value of the score is the same as the response number (e.g. if you responded 5 to item 8 then your score for that item is 5).

The following items should be reverse scored: 3, 6, 7, 9, 10 and 11 (e.g. if you responded 2 to item 7 then your score for that item is 4; if you responded 5 to item 10 then your score for that item is 1).

Go through your list of scores and mark their value (preferably in a different colour). When this is complete add up your scores (by adding the value of responses for each item) and note this.

The higher your total score, the more NEGATIVELY you view career change, by emphasizing the barriers to change rather than the factors likely to help you to change. The lower your total score the more POSITIVELY you view career change by stressing the factors most likely to assist change rather than the barriers to change.

If you have added any items of your own, you may score these in a similar way by comparing the statement with those pre-scored. If your additional statement is phrased in a POSITIVE way then you score by counting the response value for that item (e.g. if response to the additional item is 1 then your score for that item is 1). However, if your statement is phrased in a negative way then you reverse score the item (e.g. if your response to the additional item is 2 then your score for that item is 4).

USEFUL PUBLICATIONS

CAREER CHANGE (1987), by L. Morphy, CRAC, Cambridge, Hobsons Press.

DIRECTORY OF EDUCATIONAL GUIDANCE SERVICES FOR ADULTS, published by UDACE, available from Further Education Unit, Citadel Place, Tinworth Street, London SE11 5EH.

EQUAL OPPORTUNITIES: A CAREERS GUIDE (1987), by Ruth Miller and Anna Alston, a comprehensive careers guide published by Penguin Books, Harmondsworth.

GRADUATE EMPLOYMENT AND TRAINING, an annual publication by CRAC, Hobsons Publishing, Cambridge.

GRADUATE OPPORTUNITIES, an annual publication by Newpoint Publishing, London.

HIGHER EDUCATION – FINDING YOUR WAY (1988), by David Dixon, published by HMSO, London.

INTERVIEWING (1990), by Glynis M Breakwell, published by the British Psychological Society and Routledge Limited.

OCCUPATIONS (annual jobs directory), available from the Careers and Occupational Information Centre, Sheffield.

RETURNERS by Elizabeth Dobbie, available from CFW (Careers for Women), 4th Floor, 2 Valentine Place, London SE1 8QH. Telephone 0171 401 2280.

RETURN TO WORK – EDUCATION AND TRAINING FOR WOMEN (1987), compiled by the Women Returners Network and published by the Longman Group, Harlow.

SAFELY THROUGH THE FRANCHISE MAZE (1990) by Ray Childs, available from The Franchise Shop Limited, 6 Old Hillside Close, Winchester, Hampshire, SO22 5LW. Telephone Winchester (01962) 55530.

SECOND CHANCES (1987) by Andrew Pates and Martin Good (adult education and training opportunities), available from the Careers and Occupational Information Centre, Sheffield.

STARTING YOUR OWN BUSINESS (1986), a practical guide to self-employment published by the Consumers Association, London.

THE DIRECTORY OF FURTHER EDUCATION (annual courses directory), published by the Careers Research and Advisory Centre,

Hobsons Publishing, Cambridge

THE FRANCHISE DIRECTORY, available from Franchise World, 37 Nottingham Road, London SW17 7EA. Telephone: 0181 767 1371.

THE JOB BOOK (annual directory of employment and training organizations), published by CRAC, Hobsons Publishing, Cambridge.

THE SUNDAY TIMES GOOD CAREERS GUIDE by Peter Wilby, Granada Publishing.

WORKING IN (careers guidance booklets), available from the Careers and Occupational Information Centre, Sheffield.

CLASSIFICATION OF OCCUPATIONS

The following list of occupations is not exhaustive but serves to provide examples of the main occupational groups within each field. They are listed alphabetically for easy reference.

HEALTH, DENTISTRY AND MEDICINE

Ambulance staff
Chiropodist
Clinical Psychologist
Dental Hygienist
Dental Receptionist
Dental Surgery Assistant
Dental Technician
Dentist
Dietician
Dispensing Optician
Doctor
Health Visitor
Hospital Porter
Hospital Administrator
Hospital Receptionist
Laboratory Technician
Midwife
Nurse
Nursing Auxiliary
Occupational Therapist
Ophthalmic Optician
Orthoptist
Osteopath/Chiropractor
Pathologist
Pharmacist
Physiotherapist
Psychiatrist
Psychiatric Social Worker
Public and Environmental Health
Radiographer
Speech Therapist
Stress Management Consultant

AGRICULTURE & RELATED FIELDS

Agricultural Worker
Agricultural Machinery
Conservation and Ecology
Countryside Management
Crop Protection Officer
Farmer
Farm Management
Fishing
Fisheries Management
Food Management
Food Manufacture
Food Safety Management
Irrigation Engineer
Irrigation Management
Poultry Worker

Rural Recreation/Tourism
Soil/Water Engineer
Tree Surgeon
Veterinary Medicine

SCIENCE AND ENGINEERING

Biologist
Biochemist
Chemist
Electrical Engineer
Environmental Management
Geographer
Geologist
Mechanical Engineer
Physicist
Quality Control
Road Safety Engineering
Surveyor
Systems Engineering
Systems Management
Telecommunications
Technician
Textile Engineer
Transport Engineer
Water Technologist
Water Management

ARCHITECTURE, BUILDING & PLANNING

Architect
Bricklayer
Building Technician
Building Surveyor
Carpenter
Cartographer
Construction Management
Draughtsperson

Electrician
Estimator
Environmental Design
Housing Officer
Landscape Designer
Landscape Management
Painter and Decorator
Plasterer
Plumber
Quantity Surveying
Site Manager
Town & Country Planning

BUSINESS/ADMINISTRATION

Accounting & Finance
Actuary
Administrator
Advertising Copy Writer
Clerical Worker
Computer Analyst
Computer Operator
Consultant
Data Processing Operator
Insurance Advisor
Insurance Agent
Insurance Underwriter
Investment Analyst
Loss Adjuster
Marketing
Market Researcher
Personal Assistant
Personnel Officer
Public Relations Officer
Receptionist
Secretary
Stockbroker
Systems Analyst
Telephonist
Training Officer
Typist

MANUFACTURING

Baker
Foundry Worker
Engineering Operator
Fitters
Industrial Technician
Machinist
Packer
Production Manager
Production Supervisor
Production Worker
Sheet Metal Worker
Technician
Transport Worker
Transport Manager
Vehicle Mechanic
Welder

CATERING, HOTEL & RECEPTION

Chef/Cook
Domestic Staff
Entertainer
Fast Food Worker
Fitness Instructor
Home Economist
Hotel/Housekeeper
Hotel/Catering Manager
Kitchen staff
Leisure Manager
Porter
Reception staff
Swimming Bath Attendant
Waiting Staff

EDUCATION

Administrator/Manager
Advisor
Caretaker
Classroom Assistant
Lecturer
Psychologist
Researcher
Student
Teacher

ARTISTIC/CREATIVE

Animator
Archaeologist
Archivist
Artist
Art Historian
Author
Beautician
Camera Technician
Choreographer
Craft Worker
Dancer
Director
Drama Coach/Tutor
Editor
Fashion Designer
Fashion Model
Hairdresser
Image Consultant
Jewellery Designer
Journalist
Lighting Technician
Make-up Artist
Museum Worker
Musician
Photographer
Playwright
Potter
Printmaker
Professional Sportsperson

Public Relations Work
Publisher
Sculptor
Set Designer
Singer
Sound Technician
Stage Designer
Stage Manager
Video Producer
Window Dresser

SOCIAL/COMMUNITY WORK

Careers Advisor
Charity Worker
Community Worker
Education Welfare Officer
Nursery Nurse
Probation Officer
Religious Minister
Residential Care Worker
Residential Social Worker
Social Worker
Youth Worker

SAFETY/SECURITY WORK

Armed Forces
Fire Worker
Health and Safety Worker
Police
Security Advisor
Security Guard
Trading Standard Officer

DISTRIBUTION AND SALES

Agent
Demonstrator
Driver
Marketing Manager
Market Research Interviewer
Party Plan Sales Agent
Retail Buyer
Sales Assistant
Sales Manager
Sales Representative
Stores Supervisor
Stores Worker
Telesales Worker
Warehouse Worker

USEFUL ADDRESSES

The British Franchise Association
Franchise Chambers
Thames View
Newtown Road
Henley-on-Thames
Oxfordshire RG9 1HG
Tel: 01491 578049/578050

The Franchise Association
Abbey House
2 Moor Street
Ormskirk
Lancashire L39 2XN
Tel: 01695 574339

The Metropolitan Authorities
Recruitment Agency (METRA)
Box 1540
Homer Road
Solihull B91 3QB
Tel: 0121 704 6699

Alliance Against Ageism
in Employment
c/o Age Concern England
Astral House
1268 London Road
London SW16 4ER
Tel: 0181 679 8000

The 45 Network
395 Barlow Road
Altrincham
Cheshire WA14 5HW
Tel: 0161 941 2902

Enterprise Training
Freepost
TK 895
Brentford
Middlesex TW8 8BR
Tel: 01800 300 727

Small Firms Unit
Confederation of British Industry
Centre Point
103 New Oxford Street
London WC1 1DU
Tel: 0171 379 7400

The Equal Opportunities
Commission
Overseas House
Quay Street
Manchester M3 3HN
Tel: 0161 833 9244

Careers for Women (CFW)
4th Floor
2 Valentine Place
London SE1 8QH
Tel: 0171 401 2280

Business and Professional Women
UK Limited (BPW)
23 Ansdell Street
Kensington
London W8 5BN
Tel: 0171 938 1729

CAADE (Campaign Against Age
Discrimination in Employment)
395 Barlow Road
Altrincham
Cheshire WA14 5HW
Tel: 0161 941 2902

The Forties Plus Initiative
1 Ely Close
New Malden
KT3 4LG
Tel: 0181 942 4831

Small Firms Service
Business and Enterprise Branch
Employment Department
Steel House
Tothill Street
London SW1H 9NF
Tel: 01800 222999

Women in Enterprise
26 Bond Street
Yorks WF1 2PQ
Tel: 01924 361789

INDEX